Praise for Quail Bell

"The third issue of Quail Bell, from Richmond, Virginia, also contains numerous short essays, here focusing on Baltimore and Washington, DC. One particularly memorable work looks at the DC neighborhood of Anacostia, gentrification, and the current state of DC's Old Town; another goes inside offbeat spaces in Baltimore. There's some humor as well — for whatever reason, Victorian street urchin humor is a sort of comedic gift that keeps on giving. And there's a good-sized visual arts component here, too, from a collection of drawings to some beautiful photos of a small town near Guadalajara, to an interview with photographer Alexander C. Kafka. In the end, Quail Bell felt like the record of a tightly-knit community; time will tell what else emerges."

–Tobias Carroll, Vol. 1 *Brooklyn*

"[The second issue of] Quail Bell is a lovely, perfect-bound publication helmed by Christine Stoddard that features a mixture of fiction, essay, and memoir writing, side by side with grayscale art. Deceptively beautiful in its presentation, there's a dark subversiveness that runs through the content with discussions on Countess Bathory, Greek sex practices and haunted cities. It's a capital-**R** Romantic vision brought to print, and one that's well worth seeking out."

–Tenebrous Kate, *Love Train for the Tenebrous Empire*

AIRBORNE

An Anthology of The Real
BY QUAIL BELL MAGAZINE

Featuring Stories from 2010-2012

Compiled by Julie DiNisio

BELLE ISLE BOOKS

ISBN 978-1-9399301-0-1
LCCN 2013949684

Edited by Jade Miller, Julie DiNisio, and Christine Stoddard
Designed by Kristen Rebelo
Thanks to Sean Marks

Quail Bell Magazine
P. O. Box 4844
Richmond, Virginia 23220
www.quailbellmagazine.com

Published by

BELLE ISLE BOOKS
www.belleislebooks.com

We dedicate this book to all of our favorite fledglings—the ones who adore the imaginary, the nostalgic, and the otherworldly as much as we do.

~ The Quail Bell Crew

TABLE OF CONTENTS

FOREWORD

D ear fledglings,

Thank you for picking up *Quail Bell Magazine*'s inaugural book project (whether you actually bought it or are just flipping through it in the back of the bookstore.). This anthology originated as a single book filled with The Quail Bell Crew's' favorite pieces that have run on our online magazine over the past couple of years. But sometimes you lay one egg and two chicks come out. That situation emerged here, too.

When I first started *Quail Bell Magazine* as a small, personal blog in 2010, The Real vs. The Unreal was one of its key features and remain so today, though the two categories eventually evolved into separate blogs on the site. Readers and contributors often tell me that this element of the website's design is what initially piqued their interest—and kept them coming back. Naturally, when Jade Miller, Julie DiNisio, and I set down to edit this book, we had to honor the Quail Bell tradition of experimentation. And thus we toyed and ultimately settled upon cobbling together two anthologies that explore the real and unreal aspects of "the imaginary, the nostalgic, and the otherworldly."

Whether you're holding *Airborne* (The Real) or *The Nest* (The Unreal), I hope you'll have a chance to check out the companion anthology, as well. If you're not already familiar with *Quail Bell Magazine*—a website dedicated to the arts, literature, history, folklore, and other oddities—please hop on over to www.quailbellmagazine.com. We update the website daily and also print a quarterly just for the heck of it. Because what's better than pixels? Paper!

Here's a toast to words and letters and dreams. They've been the stuff of *Quail Bell*'s magic since the very beginning, and hopefully will continue to be, far into the future. Thanks to our loyal readers for all the love, generosity, and, of course, page views.

Feathery hugs,

Christine Stoddard, August 2013
Founder and Editor
Quail Bell Magazine
www.quailbellmagazine.com

HORROR FILM: A MOVEMENT

BY HELEN GEORGIA STODDARD

All right, fledglings, here's a little history lesson on the weirdness of horror films. Put on your scholar feathers and start reading:

1890s–1930s

As World War I continued, Europeans sought a fresh artistic outlook on life and ended up pursuing this vision in the forms of cinema, architecture, and painting—especially in northern and central Europe. Thus, the Expressionist movement began with a bang.

In cinema, German Expressionism was born, reaching its peak in Berlin in the 1920s. Some of the first Expressionist films are largely known for their geometric, nonrealistic sets and themes of madness, insanity, and torture. One of the most influential German Expressionist films of the horror movement is Robert Wiene's *The Cabinet of Dr. Caligari*, known for its extreme geometric set and plot twist. However, the overly nonrealistic Expressionist films were only popular for a short period until the German Expressionist movement simply died (Dickos).

Yet Expressionism was integrated into newer genres, like horror and film noir. The horror film movement was highly influenced by German Expressionism for several reasons. First, the themes of madness, insanity, and torture were mimicked. In horror films, however, these themes were intensified. Early horror films were based on gothic, known tales, first written in plays or novels. Prominent characters included Dracula, Frankenstein's monster, Jekyll and Hyde, Werewolf or Wolfman, and King Kong, all of whom are still popularized in today's cinema.

One of the earliest silent horror films was F. W. Murnau's *Nosferatu* (1922), which institutionalized the idea of vampires being sexually aggressive in their seductive nature; *Dracula* (1931) followed suit.

Something about *Dracula* compelled viewers, something intangible: "If Dracula symbolizes the unconscious pleasure that such a relationship conjures up retroactively, he also represents the terror of separation and the horror of the realization of the social meaning of that separation: subjectively, castration and mortality" (Humphries). Bram Stoker's *Dracula*, later made into a film by Tod Browning and Karl Freund, was horror's defining film, having joined up with the Universal Picture Company.

Universal promoted and popularized the horror film in the 1930s, especially with the already mentioned *Dracula* (1931) and *Frankenstein* (1931). Other films created with undertones of gothic science fiction, such as James Whale's *The Invisible Man* (1935) and Tod Browning's controversial *Freaks*, added to the substance upon which horror film thrived: thrill yet seriousness. Actors of the time, such as Bela Lugosi (Count Dracula) and Boris Karloff (Frankenstein's creation), successfully built their entire acting careers around horror.

Before sound, between the 1890s and 1920s, horror films were made through Universal and smaller picture companies alike. However, the ones not created by Universal were usually dismissed by critics and audiences, due to how successfully Universal took over the industry. One of the most accredited non-Universal films of the silent horror era is Georges Méliès's 1896 production of *Le Manoir du Diable* (The House of the Devil). In 1910, Edison Studios made the first film version of Frankenstein, which was lost for many years, only to be found and rereleased in 1993 by film collector Alois Felix Dettlaff, Sr. Notable horror films from the 1920s include *The Phantom of the Opera* (1923) and *Dr. Jekyll and Mr. Hyde* (1920).

1940s–1960s

Popular films of this type include Howard Hawk's *The Thing from Another World* (1951) and Don Siegel's *Invasion of the Body Snatchers* (1956). Meanwhile, the eminent British film company, Hammer Film Productions, was busy making "huge international successes from full-blooded technicolor films involving classic horror characters" such as sequels to *Frankenstein* (Worland). Films that portrayed ghosts and monsters in the supernatural, demonic sense, were also becoming popular; a good example is Roman Polanski's *Rosemary's Baby* (1968).

One of the most influential films of the horror film movement is George A. Romero's *Night of the Living Dead* (1968). Romero's zombie film blended "psychological insights with gore [making it] culturally, historically or aesthetically significant enough to be preserved by the United States National Film Registry" (Worland). It was also a step in the Armageddon horror sub-genre, alongside Alfred Hitchcock's *The Birds* (1963).

1970s–1980s

The positive turnout of demonic-based films of the 1960s brought a string of equally successful films, but this time, with more "evil children" undertones. Think *The Exorcist* (1970), *The Omen* (1976), and *Alice, Sweet Alice* (1976). A great deal of the youth involved in the counterculture movement had an interest in horror film. Films such as *Texas Chainsaw Massacre* (1974) spoke of the Vietnam War while Romero's sequel to *Night of the Living Dead*, called *Dawn of the Dead* (1978), dealt with the sabotage of consumerist society.

Stephen King played a large role in the horror film movement as films were quickly made off his novels. Brian De Palma's *Carrie* (1976) was King's film adaptation debut, earning many Academy Awards. *The Shining* (1980), a Stanley Kubrick film, was slow at the box office but has now been claimed a classic cult film and one of the most horrific (Worland). *Halloween* (1978), *Friday the 13th* (1980), and *A Nightmare on Elm Street* (1984) were all placed under the "slasher film" sub-genre. In 1975, Steven Spielberg brought us *Jaws*, which inspired several violent killer animal films to the screen.

1990s–present day

Sequels to *A Nightmare on Elm Street, Child's Play, Halloween,* and *Friday the 13th* were the first horror films to hit the theaters with success in the new decade. *Silence of the Lambs* was also hugely successful (1991). A minimovement arose, known as metafictional horror, which connected real-world horror with fictional horror. Films such as *Candyman* (1992) and *Scream* (1996) are good examples. *Interview with a Vampire* (1994) ushered in the Grand Guignol style, known for its naturalistic, amoral horror (Hand).

Horror film has progressed in a somewhat hideous direction, leaving its once moralistic ideas behind; many of today's horror films are merely insipid. However, from classic horror, we get a sense of romantic, erotic, and abstract thinking (which evolved from German Expressionism). It helped push forward a creative level within cinema and society as well as give answers and truth to the unknown and the terrifying. It helped play with our emotions and their extremes. The horror film movement has added a sincere piece to an otherwise empty body, hungry for adrenaline.

HISTORIC HOTSPOT: SAVANNAH, GA

BY JULIE DINISIO

The holidays are about over, and for many readers, the cold is starting to feel less cheery and more chapping. What can a Quail Bell(e) do but ruffle up her feathers and hermit herself in the house? Migrating down South to get some culture is always an option, and Savannah, Georgia, does not fail as an historic hotspot. Granted, Georgia isn't known for its balmy winter weather, but right now Savannah is roughly sixty degrees, the makings of a comparative heat wave if you're stuck in, say, New York.

Savannah is a petite, character-filled city that was founded in 1733 by James Oglethorpe, a British social reformer intent on giving debtors a second chance through settling in America. It became a royal colony less than twenty years later and acted as Georgia's capital for a while.

This genteel city is home to the South's first public art museum, the Telfair Museum of Art, which was founded in 1886 by prominent citizen Mary Telfair. Since then, buildings have been added to the original, and the museum itself plays host to a substantial collection of European and African-American works of art. Savannah also celebrates First African Baptist Church, the (arguably) oldest black church in North America, which played a large part in the Underground Railroad during the Civil War.

Savannah is a notable addition to the annals of American architecture. In its historic district, you will find a beautiful neighborhood noted for its late nineteenth-century Victorian homes, all ornate and colorful. They're almost guaranteed to make you jealous that you don't own one. And about ten miles south of Savannah is the Wormsloe Historic Site, acres of land that were once favored by a beautiful eighteenth-century plantation. There is also a famous oak-lined walkway, both charming and eerie in that impossible-to-duplicate Southern way.

Finally, if the thought of a ghost-sighting thrills you, Savannah is alleged to be a city replete with paranormal activity. Consider staying at the historic 17 Hundred 90 Inn, Room 204, where a young woman, who flung herself out the window in life, still haunts the room. Another haunted (and absolutely gorgeous) hotel is the Kehoe House, where the reported ghost interactions have never been malignant, but rather familial and endearing.

On an unrelated note, this home was purchased in the 1980s by football star Joe Namath, who had plans of turning it into a nightclub. Citizens of Savannah were outraged at the potential defilement of a landmark, and Namath never acted. This should be plenty of proof that the citizens of Savannah fiercely respect the sanctity of their city, making it a true historic hotspot.

FROM SUGGESTIVE
JESTERS TO SEXY CIRCUSES
BY PAISLEY HIBOU

A European monarch, wearing plush velvets as he melts into a glittering throne, nearly chokes on his bon-bon. Jesters are not supposed to do that. The jingling fool has started flossing with his marotte, turning his mock scepter into an undeniable phallic symbol. Then the strip tease begins. The only PG-13 sight in the room is a rumpled motley patterned frock lying on the marble floor. Harps and lutes suddenly lend the scene a suggestive sound track.

Does this episode seem perversely unreal? You might be shocked (or pleased) to learn there's a modern-day equivalent. It's called clown porn, and somewhere, someone's watching it this very second. In fact, a Google search for the term "clown porn" pulled up 1,760,000 results on November 15, 2011. A YouTube search for the same term pulled up 2,320 results on November 29, 2011. On October 30, 2011, an episode of *Family Guy* featured about twelve seconds satirizing clown porn—ironic considering that clown porn itself satirizes the porn industry. It's like the famous magic trick that features a scarf within a scarf except that Family Guy brought clown porn to mainstream attention by positioning a joke within a joke.

Maybe that joke's too meta for some folks' taste. Even so, it sparked Quail Bell's curiosity. As generic porn continues to proliferate across the Internet, so does clown porn. On December 16, 2011, a Google search for the term "clown porn" pulled up 1,880,000 results.

Given the extinction of European court life, licensed fools don't really prance around trumpeting societal follies anymore. We do, however, have the funny guys with multi-colored wigs, baggy clothes, and garish face paint to serve the same purpose. We also have the strange world of porn.

Today clowns and porn stars coexist in twisted harmony, but only because one chooses to poke fun at the other.

Porn has gotten absurd and clowns aren't afraid to say it or at least imply it. Clown porn points to our society's troubled obsession with women who fail to look like real women. At this time in history, the dysmorphic definition of the ideal babe is more contorted than ever. Elizabeth I had extreme hairline tweezing; Marie Antoinette had mouse skin eyebrows; Marilyn Monroe had bullet bras; today's porn stars are victims of Botox, laser hair removal, collagen injections, vaginal lifts, and anal bleaching.

The type of sex female porn stars portray is male-centric and, more often than not, demeaning to women. Many of the porn stars in Internet videos appear to be in pain; often you'll see them crying. The typical male co-star calls his female co-star crude names, fails to make eye contact with her, and does not abide by her wishes. That is, if the male co-star is visible at all. Often he's just a pair of hands and an anonymous penis. Not very Mr. Darcy.

The standards of beauty imposed upon female porn stars affect real women. LA Weekly ran an article in May 2011 about a study conducted by The American Society of Plastic Surgeons in time for Mother's Day. According to the study, 62% of the 1,000+ mothers surveyed said that if cost were not a factor, they would opt for a "mommy makeover," meaning a tummy tuck and a boob job. In the Renaissance and Victorian Ages, mommies were considered hotties because of their voluptuousness. More importantly, mommies had society's respect because they were bringers of life. Now, mommies feel ashamed of their bodies.

Porn star standards of "perfect" sex affect real women (and men), too. In February 2011, AARP ran an article titled "6 Ways Porn Can Hurt Your Sex Life: Viewing explicit content gives men unrealistic view of sexual performance, intimacy." Number six on the list discounted the myth that porn perpetuates: "Porn is all about hardcore action." The article quoted sex therapist Dennis Sugrue for the following: "Pornography ignores whole-body sensuality. That's a big reason why porn-style sex isn't satisfying. That's also a big reason why so many women hate it."

Bottom line: Most of today's porn presents disgusting fantasies. Clown porn shows just how fantastical those fantasies are.

Clowns are so ridiculous-looking, they have society's permission to behave in a ridiculous, even fantastical, manner. They can honk bicycle horns as a means of speech or slam overly-creamed pies in their friends' faces. Twenty of them can fit into a teeny car meant to accommodate only one or two non-clowns.

That's why clowns can get away with absurdity in porn. They can get it on in a room full of balloon animals or on a moon bounce with circus music playing in the background. They can put a female porn star in a neon green wig and white face and have her talk in goofy voices. They can even throw cream pies at each other as they perform the same crass acts common to mainstream porn. If you don't understand how half-baked today's mainstream porn is, clown porn promises to teach you.

As funny as clowns are, they're also scary. Clowns don't even have to pick up a chain saw or gun to scare some audiences. All they have to do is be themselves. Coulrophobia refers to the fear of clowns, which is so rampant that haunted houses and horror films sometimes pick clowns over ghosts and zombies. A bunch of clowns can make mainstream porn look frightening. When's the last time a porno mentioned birth control, condoms, STDs, abortions, or the cost of childcare? Never, and that's frightening.

Much of today's porn is ridiculous looking but not because it has society's explicit green card like clowns do. Internet porn has evolved from our warped values. Internet porn says that we don't want our women to look like women. We don't want our men present as anything but phallic symbols. We don't want sex to involve love or even plain ol' intimacy. Internet porn says that we want sex to be fast, impersonal, and at times cruel. It says that we want sex to take place between two non-humans: 1) a caricature of a highly-sexed little girl with alien body parts and 2) an unusually large penis wagging through the air. This is not the stuff of risque daguerreotypes.

Very few people would express these sexual values, even privately to themselves, and yet Internet porn suggests that these are the criteria viewers demand. Not many people are acting to challenge such values. If anything, they are encouraging them.

In December 2009, The Telegraph ran an article about a study of young male porn users conducted by the University of Montreal. Out of the twenty heterosexual male college students interviewed for the study, all of them used porn, a habit that, on average, started at age ten. Ninety percent of their porn came from the Internet. On average, men in relationships watched porn 1.7 times a week for about twenty minutes. As you'd probably suspect, single men watched porn more frequently and for longer durations: forty minutes, three times a week. Watching porn is a major pastime and most people won't give it up for the sake of re-defining sexual values.

The Telegraph ran another article in January 2010, this time on a study that found that men who began watching porn as boys under age sixteen were more likely to deem sexual harassment acceptable. The leader of this study held at the Australian Research Centre in Sex, Health and

Society was Michael Flood. The Telegraph quoted Flood as saying, "Porn is a very poor sex educator because it shows sex in unrealistic ways and fails to address intimacy, love, connection, or romance. Often it is quite callous and hostile in its depictions of women."

But porn hasn't always been so "callous" and "hostile." History has shown us that porn can exhibit healthy standards of beauty and good sex.

For a candid look at porn dating back to the Roaring Twenties, for instance, check out the French book *Les Années Folles des Maison Closes* by Christian Marmonnier and Alex Varenne. Regardless of whether or not you can overcome the language barrier, flip through the pages and study the photographs. Since the photos present natural, "artistic" shots, chances are the librarian sneaking up behind you won't call you a pervert.

This 143-page coffee table book depicts women with breasts that range from mosquito bites to jugs. Many of these models have rolls of fat, wrinkles, pale complexions, dark tresses, untoned bodies, and even a little body hair. Not one of these women is portrayed as ugly or odd, indicating a fairly lenient definition of beauty (though there's little in the way of ethnic and racial diversity). Very few, if any of these women, would pass muster in today's porn industry. They do not have bleached blonde hair, balloon breasts, orange tans, all-over waxes, and the tell-tale scars of plastic surgery. They are just pretty, everyday women.

Maybe porn won't ever return to the days where donning red lipstick was as scandalous as you could get. Maybe porn will continue getting skeezier and skeezier: more revoltingly fantastical and more damaging to women's self-esteem. But at least clown porn reminds us of the skeeziness.

BOPPING WITH BETTY BOOP

BY LUNA LARK

The dark, coiffed bob. Peepers the size of bagels. Shapely legs. Pouty rosebud lips. Helen Kane's Bronx baby doll voice. Teeny feet in teeny heels. Coke Bottle curves. A scandalously tight red dress. A habit of breaking out into song and dance routines at any point in time.

These traits are what make Betty Boop America's beloved Betty. She may not cater to mainstream audiences the way she did in the 1930s, but Betty still roams in the memories of the many who grew up watching her cartoons from the Great Depression into the 1990s. I include myself in that category.

As a little girl, I did not fall for Betty for the same reasons that instantly attract her male fans. I fell for her cute quirks, genuine nature, vintage glamour, and the fact that she belonged to Max Fleischer's cast of flamboyant characters.

My earliest memories of Betty Boop go back to my parents' blue Mazda MPV. My mother would prop up a small TV between the console and the back passenger's seat so my sisters and I could all watch the cartoons together on long car rides. During daylight hours, my sisters and I read and drew, but once darkness fell, we fled from the Information Age to the '30s and '40s, thanks to the magic of VHS tapes.

Those VHS tapes often showcased a hodgepodge of creations from Fleischer, Warner Brothers, Paramount, and Disney. Along with Betty, my sisters and I got a healthy dose of "Felix the Cat," "Popeye the Sailor," "Looney Tunes," "Superman," "Casper the Friendly Ghost," and "Little Lulu," among numerous others. Yet for every "Bugs Bunny" or "Little Audrey" cartoon I enjoyed, I still preferred Betty. She has spunk and something I could not articulate at the time: sex appeal. Gags, great music, and an overall decadence of visual detail helped me connect not only to Betty but to her world.

Betty cartoons I will never forget include "Bimbo's Initiation," "Bimbo's Express," "Boop-Oop-a-Doop," and "Betty Boop's Crazy Inventions." My favorite Betty cartoon remains "Snow-White" (1933), which famously features the music of Cab Calloway and the kooky animation of one-man-band Roland C. Crandall.

Despite the campiness apparent in many of these cartoons, when I was a child, Betty seemed like a better version of Barbie. Betty, though highly sexualized, is relatively independent. She lives her own life without a man, working various jobs and continually re-inventing herself. Betty could be a showgirl or an aunt or a princess or an anthropomorphized canine. She can flirt and she can dress, too. My elementary-school self admired her racy get-ups, right down to Betty's heart-shape necklines and exposed garter straps. I never cast moral judgement. I only wondered why more women did not embrace her jazzy flair.

Even today, almost two decades later, my relationship with Betty Boop continues. I occasionally return to my favorite cartoons and read up on her in books and blogs. A couple of years ago, I found an eccentric store in Alexandria, Virginia, that sold classic comic books and Venus flytraps. In addition to buying *Archie* and *Casper the Friendly Ghost* comic books, I bought a few pages from different Betty calendars printed in the '80s. One print shows Betty as a geisha; another shows her as a Parisian at an outdoor cafe. I also have depictions of Betty in Venice, Spain, and the Middle East.

Today the pages hang in my bedroom on their very own wall. They remind me of the thrill of being Betty Boop—beautiful, sophisticated (but never snobby), and full of heart.

HISTORIC HOTSPOT: LAWRENCE, KS

BY STARLING ROOT

S ometimes a Midwestern history-lover can feel left out. American history books and professors tend to focus on the coasts, not the so-called fly-over states. Pennsylvania, Virginia, Maryland, Massachusetts, New York, Texas, and California pretty much always get their names printed in big letters on the playbill while places like North Dakota and Wisconsin usually get bit parts. Even Illinois doesn't get much attention in the average high school history course. Despite their few spotlights on the main stage, Midwestern states have nonetheless helped make "America: The Musical" the ballet/rodeo show it is.

Though Boston and New Orleans are obvious destinations, Quail Bell(e)s will also find gems in the plains and prairies. One lesser-known choice is Lawrence, Kansas. Home to the main campus of the University of Kansas, Lawrence offers historic territory with definite college town appeal less than half an hour away from the state capital.

Founded in 1854 by anti-slavery Free-Staters, Lawrence has exciting Antebellum and Civil War histories. The Sacking of Lawrence—a pro-slavery group's attack on the Free-State Hotel and two abolitionist newspapers—came in 1856. Not far from the town, abolitionist John Brown led the Pottawatomie Massacre in 1856, as well. In 1863, the Lawrence Massacre, headed by Confederate guerrilla William Clarke Quantrill, resulted in the burning of many local buildings and the death of 150 men. Then in 1865, Lawrence residents established the University of Kansas with the help of a charter granted by the Kansas Legislature and land donation by Kansas' former governor. And these events are but the early highlights! During WWII, the federal government even set up an internment camp for German and Italian prisoners in Lawrence.

Lawrence lays claim to not one, not two, but several historic districts:

Downtown, Pinckney #1, Pinckney #2, North Rhode Island, South Rhode Island, Hancock, Old West Lawrence, Breezedale, East Lawrence, and Oread. (For a population shy of 88,000, that's quite a list.) These districts have been recognized by the Lawrence Register of Historic Places, the Register of Historic Kansas Places, and the National Register of Historic Places.

According to the National Trust for Historic Preservation, Lawrence ranks among the "Dozen Most Distinctive Destinations" for well-preserved, diverse historic communities. The city's main strip lies on Massachusetts Street, where you can see Liberty Hall, Eldridge Hotel, Miller's Hall, The House Building, Sunflower, Ernst Hardware, Watkins Community Museum, and the Douglas County Courthouse. On Alabama Street, you'll also find the boyhood home of black poet Langston Hughes.

Apart from visiting these historic sites, Quail Bell(e)s should see any of the city's 12 art galleries, grab a meal at Johnny's Tavern, watch a show at Jackpot Music Hall, attend a Kansas basketball game, or check out the university's highly regarded performing arts center. In the summertime, you might catch the Downtown Lawrence Film Festival or Lawrence Busker Fest.

With so much history and art peppering the city, Lawrence, Kansas, should not be overlooked, despite its fly-over status.

VIRGINIA'S VINTAGE HAPPY CAPITAL

BY CHRISTINE STODDARD

Fashionistas come in all forms, including self-proclaimed '50s sit-com dads with day jobs at universities. Their glasses run thick, their ties blink black, and their pants come in only one variety: business professional. If images of Milanese catwalk-worshipping cadavers are still haunting you, meet the outlier—Southern fashionista Brian McDaniel, founder of the popular street and lifestyle blog, DirtyRichmond.tumblr.com.

This fast-talking gentleman captures flashes of Richmond, Virginia's distinctive fashion and social scenes on the digital camera he normally has slung around his shoulder. In a place where "the city is dirty but the people are not" and art and history often collide, Brian's inspiration is as likely to trot on sidewalks as it is to party in Edwardian-era row houses. Following in the footsteps of The Sartorialist and Bill Cunningham, Brian instinctively photographs what compels him in the moment.

Brian jump-started Dirty Richmond (commonly called Dirty RVA for short) in September 2009, after spending a semester studying business in Hong Kong. While he had hoped Hong Kong would offer the same kind of over-the-top fashion rampant in Tokyo, Brian found the common street style there more conservative. He often found himself nostalgically describing Richmond, the historic city not far from his native suburban Chesterfield County. The city's also home to his alma mater, Virginia Commonwealth University, well-known for its art and communications programs. Both the city's plethora of late nineteenth-century enthusiasts and creative undergrads contribute to Richmond's playfulness with clothes and interior design.

Brian's frequent documentation of Richmond's young and dashing has given him insight into the largely vintage scene. During his recent chat with Quail Bell Magazine, Brian pointed to the "older people living in The Fan [Richmond's famous Victorian district]" as one reason for why young Richmonders dress and decorate the way they do.

Richmond, founded in 1737, is one of the oldest cities in the United States. Many families have inhabited the area for generations, in some cases since the Revolutionary War. Select older residents pride themselves on having been born and raised in the capital of the Confederacy. Relics of the Civil War still abound in monuments, street names, and museums. Long-time Richmonders of age and means sell their vintage clothes and heirlooms to boutiques like Anthill Antiques, Bygones, and Halcyon, while also donating to thrift shops like Fantastic and Diversity. Given the wealth of secondhand stores in neighborhoods like the Fan and Carytown, a young person living in RVA doesn't have to be rich to afford these gems.

Young Richmonders also don't have to be particularly observant to see vintage fashion in historically-accurate action. To illustrate the way tradition lives on in old-timers' fashion, Brian explained how Sundays in predominantly black neighborhoods like Carver and Jackson Ward mean the elderly deck themselves out in "really fantastic outfits" from their heydays. This usually means the 1960s, when most Richmond women still wore hats to church and gloves still adorned many hands. In the white community, with scores of Civil War re-enactment groups dressing up in and around the city, it's not entirely uncommon to spot fashion from the 1860s—Sunday or otherwise. Brian stated that while he has not yet photographed a Civil War re-enactor, he'd love to do so.

As for what's in with the young and stylish of Richmond right now? Brian praised vintage dresses, men's hats, and '70s facial hair as current big things. He noticed that most young Richmonders, even the bold and artsy, don't fully embrace vintage from head-to-toe, unless they happen to work at one of the aforementioned boutiques. They tend to insert a piece here or there, lest they become walking museum mannequins. A lover of classic TV shows like Dick Van Dyke, Brian calls his own look an interpretation of "vintage with a modern take."

According to Brian, the local history and architecture influence young Richmonders' home style as well.

"Space [here] is very personal," he said, applauding Richmond's near lack of cookie-cutter apartment complexes and dorms.

Richmond brims with terraced houses, porches, hardwood floors, and big windows. Many Richmond row houses feature antique furniture and home accessories. While most of these things date back decades, some date back centuries. It's not uncommon for an RVA twenty-something to add touches of Art Deco and Art Nouveau to her collection of Target furniture. Brian believes that antiques just don't mesh with buildings devoid of historic charm.

Overall, Brian thinks that "Richmond is very accepting. People here make style their own. It's nice to be able to put on anything you want and not feel weird because nobody's going to care."

And this is coming from a man whose daily vocabulary includes antiquated expressions like "Shucks!" and "Fiddlesticks!" It's no wonder he feels at ease in Virginia's vintage-happy capital.

GOOD OLD-FASHIONED
SUSPENSE

BY JULIE DINISIO

Alfred Hitchcock did not necessarily look like the master of suspense. Photos of this British director and movie industry icon remind me of an English Bulldog. Or a grumpy old man. This is a case of you can't judge a book by its cover. Hitchcock was a genius, a pioneer in film, and far more innovative than any bulldog I've ever known. He introduced previously unused camera angles and wrote stories to keep his viewers on the edge of their seats. In his lifetime, he directed over fifty movies. Below are some of the most popular and some of the more notably obscure features on Hitchcock's impressive list of accomplishments:

Rebecca (1940)
Based on Daphne du Maurier's famous novel, this movie stars Laurence Olivier and Joan Fontaine. It is a beautiful, gothic tale that subtly highlights Hitchcock's talent in dealing with the supernatural and suspenseful.

Rope (1948)
This was one of his most interesting works of filming. The story centers around two young men who strangled one of their friends to see if they could get away with murder. Almost all of the movie is shot on one set, the dining room of an apartment, and most of the scenes continuously run for ten or more minutes.

Rear Window (1954)
In a similar fashion to Rope, much of this movie takes place from one angle, the window view of one apartment. When a professional photographer, played by James Stewart, witnesses a murder, he has to piece together

the puzzle without leaving his apartment (due to a broken leg).

Vertigo (1958)
In this film, a detective confronts his fear of heights while following an al-
legedly possessed woman. Due to an unforeseeable twist, this is considered
one of the director's most defining works.

Psycho (1960)
There's no way you haven't seen this movie. I'm not even going to bother
explaining the plot. Just know that taxidermy and multiple personalities
combine in one incredibly creepy, innovative movie.

KILLER LEGS BY NYLON

BY JADE MILLER

The best thing about being a fashionable Quail Bell(e) is discovering those perfect pieces or creative ways to combine old pieces in that wardrobe into an amazing new take on an outfit. Yet in the world of fashion, what might seem original and innovative to us has actually been around for ages.

References to hosiery go all the way back to the Egyptians, who wore the first socks, and the Ancient Greeks, where workmen and slaves wore hose and Roman women wore short socks in their homes. These socks transitioned into stockings in the Middle Ages in Europe when men wore breeches and women wore stockings with garters. Also at this time, silk stockings were all the rage with heavier linen socks covering the delicate fabric when worn with boots.

Though stockings were originally created without fashion in mind, it didn't take long for them to become an expression of self. The Dandies, in the sixteenth century, layered different colors and patterns and heights of stockings and socks in order to create their personal looks.

Fast-forward to 1940 when the first nylons went on sale. All four millions pairs sold out in four days. Women don't like to mess around with naked legs, and sheer nylon stockings with a seam up the back were the epitome of sexy. All these ladies had to give up their stockings during World War II, and women used makeup on their legs and eyebrow pencils to get the look of a seam.

The next development in hosiery was in 1959 with the introduction of spandex, and from then until now, not much has changed. When looking for a pair of stockings for your very own, keep a few things in mind. The denier is the measurement for knitting, which determines how sheer the stocking is that you buy. The lighter the thread, the more fine the weave is, so 15d is more sheer than a 30d stocking. There are also opaque stockings, very popular today, if you want some something with more cover. You also need to consider if you want tights, which go up around the waist, or actual stockings, held by garter belts or by elastic at the top, like thigh highs.

To further peak your interest in stockings, wrap your mind around these fascinating hosiery facts: Nylon got its name from when it was shown at the World Fair in New York in 1939. NBA players, including Kobe Bryant, used to wear tights under their shorts for more support until tights got banned in 2006. Last but not least, Joe Namath is more famous for starring in a panty hose commercial than he is for winning the Super Bowl! How's that for fashion forward?

VOLTAIRE: NOT THE PHILOSOPHER
BUT THE TOY-MAKER

BY PAISLEY HIBOU

A urelio Voltaire Hernández—that's the opulent birth name of the dark cabaret musician whose stage name is just as beautifully old-fashioned: Voltaire. With credits in not only music, but also publishing, comics, animation, and even toys, the former wunderkind got his start in show biz animating for Parker Brothers at age seventeen. Mixing drama with satire, the multi-talented creator has earned a loyal following since Projekt Records released his first album in 1998.

Now the Cuban immigrant with Jersey roots claims icon status in New York's goth scene. Voltaire's music deviates from mainstream goth by infusing the violins and cellos of European folk sounds with poppy vocals and often whimsical lyrics. But, again, this is a man who could not be content with making music alone. Today Voltaire still performs, but he also teaches stop-motion at the School of Visual Arts in New York and continues unleashing a flurry of brain children onto the gothic scene.

In a recent interview with Quail Bell, Voltaire discussed the territory of his ever-expanding toyland:

Quail Bell: You're like a gothic da Vinci. You make music, films, books, toys, and, most famously, mayhem. Let's focus on the toys!

As an animator and cartoonist, toys seem like a natural outlet for your creations. What were some of your favorite toys as a child? How have they inspired any of your toys, if at all?

Voltaire: I was always a fan of monsters, so my favorite toys were mostly monster toys. I had some Universal Monsters action figures by MEGO that I was fond of when I was really little, and I collected these little monster figurines from a breakfast cereal called Freakies. Later on, I had a giant alien from H. R. Giger's *Alien*, and then, of course, I got into *Star Wars* action figures. But one of my earliest memories regarding toys was seeing this strange, spotted alien toy that was shrink-wrapped to a box of laundry detergent. Looking back, the monster looked a bit like Sy Snootles from *Return of the Jedi*. In any case, the only way to get this toy was to buy the detergent, and my grandmother, whom I was with at the time, was having none of it (laughs). I'll never forget that blasted alien toy, and I think that perhaps the elusive nature of it gave me a love and appreciation for obscure monster toys. The more obscure it is, especially if it's not tied to a big license, TV or film, the more mysterious and interesting it is to me.

QB: How would you define the art of toy design? Do you have a routine process?

V: To be frank, I don't have much choice when it comes to how I design toys. Most of the toys I've made have been in the world of what they call "designer vinyl" and on what they call "blank canvas" or "platform toys," which means that the shape already exists and different artists design their version of that toy.

For instance, a company like Toy2R from Hong Kong will make a vinyl figure of a bear and then they will give that same vinyl bear to a few different artists to design. Sometimes they give you the actual vinyl toy, you paint on it and then it gets sent to a factory where it's duplicated and manufactured. But usually, what I get sent is a template in Illustrator format. It's an outline of the toy from the front, back and other sides. I can then print it out and draw on it, or do all of the designing in the computer. I usually do all of the designing in Photoshop.

QB: Talk to us about your Deady character. Who is he? What's his story?

V: Deady is actually the galaxy's greatest evil, a giant tentacled skull named Urkor Malravenus who escaped confinement on the cemetery planet of Necronus and is hiding in a little teddy bear here on Earth. But that wasn't revealed to me right away, mind you. His story developed slowly over time.

I think it was back in 2002 or so that I had signed a deal with a clothing company called Mighty Fine. The idea was that I'd provide them with T-shirt designs that they could sell to stores like Hot Topic. I did some designs of a cute but evil teddy bear with snarky slogans. One said, "Just because I'm adorable doesn't mean I won't rip your face off" or something like that. Another one said, "Deady loves kids . . . well done with a little barbecue sauce."

Originally his name was Evil Teddy. But around that time, Hot Topic had told me they wouldn't accept anything with the words "hell," "devil" or "evil" in it due to growing complaints from parents in the heartland of America that felt Hot Topic was turning their children into devil worshippers! (laughs) I eventually came up with the name "Deady," and in the end, I preferred it.

I get very attached to my characters, so after drawing Deady a few times, I started to think about who he was and where he came from, imagining all sorts of adventures he's had. I got the idea to make a Deady graphic novel series so that I could tell those stories. I ended up making four books, each with forty-eight pages of art and stories about Deady. They had incredible guest artists and writers in them including Hellraiser creator Clive Barker, Neil Gaiman, Roman Dirge, Gris Grimly, James O'Barr, Tokidoki, and many other incredibly talented people. And as you already know, it eventually spun off into a line of toys.

QB: What's your favorite toy you've designed and why?

V: I don't know that I could pick a favorite. I have lots of them! I like the Deady as "Stitch" from *Lilo and Stitch* that I made with Mindstyle a couple of years ago. It's a really good looking toy, but mostly I like the idea that Disney made a Deady toy! (laughs)

I also feel really lucky to have been given an opportunity to make Hot Wheels cars. I designed a two-car set for the Japanese collector's market that included a Deady hearse and a Chi-chian Worm Wrangler truck. I can't say I ever imagined I'd get to design Hot Wheels cars!

I think my favorite toy is still out there waiting to get made. I have always wanted to make a Chi-chian action figure, and I haven't given up hope of it happening some day.

QB: On your website, you mention having so many toy companies' "doors slammed" in your face. Could you talk about some of the trials and tribulations you encountered in your early days as a toy designer?

V: Long before I'd ever made a toy, I was making comic books. My first two comic book series were *Chi-chian* and *Oh My Goth!*, and as you might imagine, they're both filled with colorful characters. Any artist who's ever grown up playing with action figures dreams of seeing their own characters become toys, and I was certainly no exception. I'd see Spider-Man toys and Batman toys in stores and I'd think, hey, I create comic books, my characters could be made into toys, too!

So I went to some of the companies making action figures back then and proposed they make figures of my characters. Everybody I spoke to was super nice and they always seemed to think my comic book characters were very interesting but no one would ever want to sign the deal to make my toys. I was constantly being rejected and no one would ever tell me why.

I had to eventually learn on my own that making toys has nothing to do with how cool or interesting or beautiful your characters are. It only matters how many people are familiar with them! It can cost around a hundred thousand dollars to put an action figure into production. The metal mold or "tool" they make to cast the plastic can cost tens of thousands of dollars on its own.

So what characters are these companies going to make figures of? Characters like Chi-chian that only a few thousand people know about? That's a very risky business. Companies want to be assured that if they spend tens of thousands of dollars, there are going to be tens of thousands or more people poised to buy the figures they make. So they make figures of characters everyone knows, characters from Hollywood movies and characters that are household names that millions of people are familiar with like Mickey Mouse and Superman and Bart Simpson and Darth Vader. It's a numbers game, plain and simple.

So the sad truth is that if you create a character and it's not in a blockbuster film or television show, you can pretty much forget about seeing it developed into a plastic action figure. I had to learn that the hard way on my own because, sadly, people just won't tell you this to your face.

QB: Now for the positive! What sort of successes have you had with your toys?

V: Well, the really brilliant thing is that just as I was giving up hope of ever seeing my characters made into toys, there was an amazing development in the toy world. About a decade ago, some enterprising artists in Hong Kong who had access to Chinese factories started hiring the factories to make vinyl toys of their designs. These characters were not from video games or blockbuster movies, they were just straight from the artists' imaginations. Since the artists didn't have a lot of money, they couldn't make millions of the toys, just a couple hundred or so. This made these toys highly collectible and very sought after.

These artists, in essence, created a new toy market that some called "urban vinyl" or "designer vinyl." Simply put, they were vinyl toys, designed by artists, made in very limited runs. Suddenly, an artist such as myself could get their characters turned into vinyl toys!

A few companies popped up that starting making designer vinyl toys. One of them is called Toy2R. They were making these little vinyl bears called "Qee." I started seeing them at my shows hanging from fan's backpacks. I went to a store here in New York City called ToyTokyo and bought a few of them. Eventually, I emailed the company. I told them who I was and what I was doing. I said, "You make vinyl bears, my character Deady is a bear—maybe we could make one together." And they agreed.

My first toy ever was a two and a half inch tall figure of Deady on a key chain made by Toy2R. That figure sold out almost immediately, and the rest is history. I've now made over a dozen different Deady toys with Toy2R alone.

QB: Deady's already prompted bootleggers! If you could have a face-to-face conversation with bootleggers, what would you tell them?

V: Well, actually I have had a talk with some bootleggers in China who were churning out Deady bootlegs and what they told me was, "This not bootleg, we no make!" When I prodded further, they insisted that by Chinese law if the character is ten percent different, then it's not a bootleg. Then they pointed out to me that the eye on the Deady bootleg they were making was a little different than the original. It's just crazy! But I suppose it should come as no surprise.

There is a Disneyland in China that is completely unlicensed by Disney! They have a Mickey Mouse and a Donald Duck and all the same characters but their names are all just a little bit different, like Mikey Mouse and Donny Duck! "It not bootleg! We no make!" (laughs)

The thing about bootlegs though, especially for a little-known artist like myself, is that it's kind of flattering. Though I don't make any money from the bootlegs, it's still kind of cool knowing that there is enough interest in my characters that a factory in China would invest time and money to rip me off. (laughs)

QB: You always seem to have new projects. What lies in your toy future?

V: I'm in full swing of what appears to be a "Deady and Fiends 5 Mini-Qee" series by Toy2r. We released a five-inch "Mini-Qee" figure of Deady called "Deady Big in Japan" back in the summer of 2011. We released three versions of this Japanese-inspired Deady figure. They each had different facial expressions and were called "Karate Kiai," "Ronin Raspberry," and "Samurai Smirk." Shortly thereafter, towards the end of summer, we released an "Urkor Malravenus" five-inch Mini-Qee.

All of these toys came with a code to unlock a digital pet in the super popular online game "Adventure Quest Worlds" where Deady and I appear as special guests every Friday the 13th. There are three Friday the thirteenths in 2012, so I'm sure Deady and I will be very busy in that game.

The next round of Deady Mini-Qees from Toy2R appear to be a line of vinyl bunnies. There's a figure of "Deady Bunee" that we are presently working on that's simply Deady as a rabbit. But we are also working on a figure of "Sleezter Bunny," one of Deady's rivals from the comic book series. I'm hoping to have the bunny figures out by Easter, of course.

I also really need to get a new Deady plush toy made. I could never keep those in stock when I had them!

QB: Lastly, what do you think makes toys so special?

V: Toys exist for the sole purpose of bringing us joy. Nothing makes a child happier than giving them a toy. They just completely light up. They feel a kind of intense, pure happiness most of us adults have forgotten how to feel. As we get older, other things take the place of toys, things like money, sex, booze, success. But some part of us deep inside still remembers the joy we felt when playing with our favorite toys. I'm reminded of Citizen Kane's last word, "Rosebud." People who can still connect with their inner child will always love toys.

P.S. Take them out of the box and play with them, dammit! (laughs)

Oh, and anyone interested in seeing more of the toys I've made, can see them at Voltaire.net/toy_gallery.

THE WALKING CORPSES OF PILGRIMS & INDIANS

BY CHRISTINE STODDARD

Blood, guts, and mayhem tinged the first* Thanksgiving just as much as they do any horror film.

Smiling construction-paper-hand turkeys hardly evoke the relief the Pilgrims felt during their first harvest season with the Wampanoag Indians. Though they arrived in Plymouth, Massachusetts, in the autumn of 1620, the majority of Pilgrims took the Mole People approach to life in the New World, and it wasn't until March that most of them emerged from their dark, dank ship! Green-complexioned and lethargic, the Pilgrims hardly had the strength to establish their new colony. By then, disease and starvation had killed half of the Mayflower's 102 original passengers. The ship stank of piss, vomit, and hopelessness. Do you see the potential for zombie stories already?

It's no wonder the Pilgrims appreciated meeting two English-speaking Indians—Squanto being the far more fluent of the two since he had lived as a slave in London for years. After he broke free of his chains and returned to America, Squanto discovered that smallpox had nearly rendered his tribe, the Patuxet, extinct. So he decided to live with the Wampanoag, whose Algonquin name means "The Dawn People." Though that, too, sounds like the premise for a zombie tale, the Wampanoag were so named because, as East Coasters, they were the first Indians to see the sunrise each morning.

Thanks to Squanto and his supporting cast of Wampanoag, the remaining Pilgrims learned the ways of the American land. Most famously, the Pilgrims picked up the stinky trick of using dead fish as fertilizer for beans and pumpkins.

In November 1621, about fifty Pilgrims and ninety Indians pigged out at a three-day feast that resulted from lots of woodsy carnage. Everything from venison to duck to turkey to shellfish to swans to eels to, yes, seals filled their rumbling tummies. Much meat was ripped from bones upon bones throughout the celebration. Aside from all that flesh, the meal featured pudding, dried berries, nuts, and other fruits, vegetables, and baked goods.

Of course centuries have passed since that fateful episode in Plymouth. Now the question is what has become of all those Pilgrims and Indians? What about all those turkeys and eels and other tasty animals, too? You may not have thought about deer and lobster spirits before, but they exist just as much as Squanto's. Imagine all of the zombies lurking over the land where the Pilgrims and Wampanoag broke bread and endured massive hangovers from wild grape wine. Picture the Pilgrims who perished on the Mayflower before it even reached Massachusetts and the others who died on the docked ship, never once stepping onto American soil.

Maybe Thanksgiving—with its own spectrum of horrors—is closer to Halloween than you ever realized.

*Which Thanksgiving came first—Newfoundland's, Virginia's, or Florida's—is still hotly contested amongst historians today.

BETTIE BANGS & POMPADOURS

BY JADE MILLER

Nothing says style and sophistication quite like a classic look, and nothing is more classic (and a little bit gothic) than the pin-up girl style of the 1950s. With Bettie Page and Rosie the Riveter as style icons, who could go wrong? The chic pompadour and elegant makeup of the rockabilly style flatter every girl.

The quintessential hairstyle of rockabilly is "Bettie Bangs." Bettie Bangs are blunt, straight bangs that lie across the forehead. This hairstyle is named after the famous Bettie Page, who really emphasized her bangs with simple, no-fuss styling for the rest of her hair. This is a simple and easy way to achieve a great rockabilly style with minimal upkeep.

Another hairstyle to try out is the quick pompadour. Using a rattail comb, gather your bangs to the front of your head and pull them up and back, twisting them to the side. Then, push the hair forward, creating the traditional pompadour pouf and pin at the end with a small clip or bobby pins. Give a hearty spritz of hair spray. You could always follow this up with a Rosie bandana tied in a double knot behind the bangs for that extra step into pure rockabilly.

As far as makeup goes, rockabilly is all about emphasizing the lips. A strong red lip is the focus of the face, while everything else is very minimal. Start by powdering your face to get a smooth surface to start with. Follow this with blush, using a quality make-up brush, swept high up on your cheekbones as opposed to the apples of your cheeks, going close to your eyes up towards your hairline. Using an angled eyeshadow brush, take a dark shadow and emphasize your eyebrows, extending the color just a bit past your natural brow. Apply black liquid liner to the top lid, adding a small cat-eye flourish, and use mascara on the top and bottom lashes. Next, enhance your eyes with white eyeliner on the water line. Use a shimmery light color on your eyelids going up to the brow with a darker brown in the lid crease to give a subtle accent. Finally, to keep your lips kissable, use a little chapstick before applying lip liner and lipstick. Make an X shape with the liner to really give your top lip "oomph," and fill in your lips with a killer red lipstick.

But what's rockabilly style without the right outfit? Think cropped cardigans, circle skirts, cat-eye glasses, and saddle shoes. When looking for vintage pieces, turn to places that are honest about the quality of their merchandise. EBay.com is never a bad place to look, and Etsy.com is always an option, too, but you can also check out RustyZipper.com. They're very good about labeling their pieces with different tags so you know what you're getting into before you buy it. Also, it never hurts to have some sewing skills, as vintage pieces will require more upkeep than the average dress you pick up at any old store. For a more updated pin-up style, or some sexy lingerie, turn to PinUpGirlClothing.com, which definitely channels the rockabilly style.

We can't forget about the guys of the 1950s either. Elvis Presley and James Dean made sexy stylish rather than taboo, and the pompadour and jeans with white tees reigned supreme. Rather than being just another guy in the hipster herd, stand out! Nothing is more attractive than a stylish man with a dash of danger, and nothing says "bad boy" like a sweet pompadour and a well-worn leather jacket.

Rockabilly hair for men is all about long in front and short in the back. Slicked back hair is always an option, or go the extra mile and do a pompadour. A pretty simple hairstyle, it just takes some pomade, a pick comb, and a little time. Start by using a heavy pomade, High Life, or Voodoo Brew, and rub it in your palms to melt it a little bit to make it easier to use. Apply this all through your hair, slicking it straight back. Using a pick comb, take that hair straight up, almost like you're going for a mohawk. With both your hand and the comb, shape your pompadour with the high front and the combed-down back. Finish the style with some long sideburns and your look is complete!

For guys' clothing, simpler is better. Skinny cut dark jeans, white tees, leather jackets, motorcycle boots, and bowling shirts really make the rockabilly look for men. If you're feeling fancy, go for a slim-fit suit with a skinny tie à la Buddy Holly.

When trying to find the right look for you, turning to the past for inspiration is often a great place to start. The '50s had some very cool trends that transfer into today's times pretty seamlessly but still manage to give you a unique style that's super fashionable.

1920s' SURVIVAL GUIDE: SPEAKEASY PROTOCOL

BY STARLING ROOT

No buts about it, you're a real classy dame with a fringed silk dress that falls at just the right length—a sexy one, with plenty of leg in the deal, not like those gals still hung up on Edwardian conservatism. Your eyes are sultry, lined better than stained glass. Your hair's perfectly bobbed. Your chest's taped flat in true tomboy fashion. It's 1922, and the United States is at the height of Prohibition (or the so-called Noble Experiment), and you're confident that strutting into any speakeasy with your killer looks and sweet-talking mouth will be a doozie.

Well, even if you're a dollface who knows how to pay a compliment or two, there are still a few things you should know about illegal drinking establishments. Here's your speakeasy survival guide:

1. Know that there's more than one name for a speakeasy. These elusive pubs also go by the names of "blind pig" and "blind tiger," though these names usually refer to blue-collar places. So next time you hear one of these terms, don't think the conversation's about livestock or wildlife!

2. Exercise your consumer choice. There are at least 30,000 speakeasies in New York City alone.

3. Study your flapper slang. Quiz: Can you define the following? Applesauce, Baloney, Bell Bottom, Berries, Big Six, Bump Off, Cheaters, Dogs, Edge, Flivver, Giggle Water, Hoofer, Iron, Mrs. Grundy, Orchid, Piker, Torpedo. If not, bury your nose in a book before you even dare set foot out of the house.

4. Practice running in your dance shoes or kicking them off. If and when the coppers come, you'd better dash and hide.

5. Pack a flask, coconut, or garden hose so you can take a little moonshine home with you.

6. You need a password (or a big bribe) to get into a speakeasy. Should you find yourself passwordless, guess! "Swordfish" is the most common one. Other probabilities include "blotto," "bug-eyed Betty," "jalopy," "Jake," "jazz baby," and "flat tire."

7. Once you're finally in a speakeasy, remember to do just that—speak easy. Don't be too loud and rowdy, lest the police invade the joint.

8. To maintain the reputation of a "good girl," stick to ordering wine.

9. Also avoid discussing women's rights. The Woman's Christian Temperance Union—one of the same groups that helped bring about Prohibition in the first place—also jumped onto the women's suffrage bandwagon. Quite frankly, some people aren't a fan of the connection. You don't want to start a fight with any of your fellow beer-chuggers.

CELEBRATE LIFE AFTER DEATH THE MEXICAN WAY

BY JADE MILLER

Day of the Dead, or El Día de los Muertos, is a Mexican holiday that has been around for centuries. In fact, it can be traced back to the Aztecs, who had a festival to celebrate the goddess Mictecacihuatl, the Queen of the Underworld. She has been represented in pictures as just a skeleton with her mouth open wide to swallow the stars during the day. It's easy to see that influence within modern Day of the Dead celebrations with skeletons peppering everything having to do with the holiday.

November 1, El Día de los Inocentes, honors children while November 2 honors adults. During the span of the holiday, which can sometimes include October 31 as well, families clean and decorate the graves of their loved ones, usually with marigolds. These flowers are thought to lead souls to the offerings, letting them leave without straying and getting stuck in limbo.

Families also set up altars, which feature the favorite foods and drinks of the departed, as well as photos and memorabilia. For examples of El Día de los Muertos altars right here in QB's native Richmond, Virginia, check out the altar for our recently deceased managing editor, Josephine Stone, at Penny Lane Pub on 5th Street. There's another one for the Harvey family at World of Mirth in Carytown.

Usually, the family will spend time at the altar, telling stories and anecdotes about the deceased. Sometimes families will spend the whole night in the cemetery at the gravesite of their loved one. To those with literary talents, writing a short poem called a "calavera" (skull) describing interesting or funny facts about the deceased is another way to honor their souls.

El Día de los Muertos is a very beautiful way to keep someone loved and lost close to your heart, and to celebrate life instead of death. There is some form of this holiday in almost every culture, and with good reason. It gives the living hope to think of loved ones having a good life after death and comfort to think of them visiting once a year.

TICK-TOCK IN OLD-TIMEY STYLE

BY THE FEATHERY FASHIONISTA ━━━

Sure, you can pull out your phone to check the time, but wouldn't you rather be all White Rabbit about it and carry something more elegantly designed for that exclusive purpose? I'm not talking wrist watches, though those can be pretty nifty throw-backs, too. Think more along the lines of steampunk glamour. The towering top hat. The swirling cape. The bug-eyed goggles. Got it yet? Yup. The pocket watch. Pocket watches are beautiful and, pardon the pun, timeless.

Pocket watches first popped up in the late 1400s/early 1500s, during a time when most clocks still lived in church towers and cathedrals. Earlier mobile watches were inaccurate, boxy objects worn around the neck or belt.

Today, historians often credit the German locksmith Peter Henlein of Nuremberg as one of the first pocket watch inventors. He thought up a hog bristle spiral spring whose winding and uncoiling would move the clock's hour hand. In fact, the hour hand was the clock's only hand at that point in history. Minute hands came about in the late 1600s.

Pocket watches first came in steel and, later on, brass, silver, and gold. It wasn't until the 1700s that English watchmakers started making protective cases for pocket watches and adding glass crystals to protect the dial.

Pocket watches remained luxury items until the late 1700s, when painted watches became available even to sailors. In 1857, Waltham (formerly known as the American Watch Company) put Model 57 on the market. This model was the first pocket watch to use standardized parts, lowering the cost of manufacturing. In the mid to late 1800s, the rise of pocket watch factories and the widespread use of railroads led to the pocket watch's ubiquity.

Sadly for pocket watch lovers, wristwatches overshadowed the popularity of pocket watches in men's fashion after World War I. Previously, society had seen wristwatches as a feminine accessory. During the war, military men realized how much more convenient it was to wear the time on your wrist than in your pocket while on the move.

Given current fashions, you might have no idea about where to find a pocket watch, or what to look for once you actually find one. Or how much to spend. You, being a Quail Bell(e), want to be an informed consumer. That's why I put together this article. Call the QB Crew your humble servants (preferably à la *A Little Princess.*)

Here are tips for buying your first (or tenth) pocket watch:

- The biggest question you must ask yourself before you embark on this adventure is this: Do you want an antique vintage watch, a replica of an antique watch, or a modern interpretation of the real deal? If you're crossing your fingers for an authentic oldie, your best bet is to look online, especially on eBay.com. As for replicas and modern versions, you can check out everything from mainstream jewelry and vintage clothing stores to costume and artisan shops to Etsy.com and more. When buying online, always inspect photographs carefully, ask questions, and be mindful of shipping costs.

- Antiquarians should always check out the watch's serial number to verify that a watch is as old as a vendor says it is. Refer to *American Watches: Beginning to End, ID & Price Guide* or *The Complete Price Guide to Watches* for details.

- Choose between an open-face or Hunter-case watch. Hunter-case watches have spring-hinged covers that protect the watch dial. Sometimes you'll find half-Hunters, too. That's a watch with a cover that has a glass panel in the middle so you can see the hands without opening the lid.

- If the look of mechanical systems excites you, consider getting a "skeleton" design. This allows you to see all the watch's inner workings move as they tick away the day.

- To chain or not to chain—that is the question. Chains were originally added to pocket watches so that gentleman could attach the watch to the front of their waistcoats or lapels. Over time, some men decided against showing off their pocket watches but opted for a chain, anyway.

- For something shorter than a chain, go for a fob. A fob is a small leather strap, which may or may not include a protective flap for the watch face. You might even decide to never wear your watch but put it in a display dome or stand instead.

- Cartoon-lovers should research character watches. A wink from Betty Boop could add a lot of charm to an already charming pocket watch. In the 1930s, Walt Disney and other cartoonists partnered with watchmaker Ingersoll to make watches that had cartoon characters on the face (and occasionally the back). Mickey Mouse, Donald Duck, Popeye, Porky Pig, and Superman are just a handful of the characters immortalized on twentieth-century pocket watches.

- Engraving a pocket watch is a relatively affordable way to date a family heirloom. Get your name and the year you acquired the watch so future generations have no doubt about who owned the little ticker.

- Pocket watches can be expensive. Again, it goes back to the big question—do you want old or new? A more expensive watch doesn't necessarily mean a "better" watch. Better is a highly subjective word when describing pocket watches because pocket watches can be so highly personalized. What one person deems a plus, another person might deem a minus.

- Regardless of what you pay, you need to know exactly what you're getting, such as a guarantee and the right to return to the watch under the vendor's stated conditions. Think carefully about what you want and start doing basic price comparisons online. Then you can see what's a reasonable price range for the specific pocket watch you have in mind.

- A few pocket watch makers include Waltham, Charles Hubert, Elgin, Ball, Dudley Masonic, Swiss Army, Hamilton, Hampden, Luminox, Illinois, Ingersoll, Patek Phillippe, Howard, RailRoad Watch, and even Harley Davidson and Ed Hardy. Walthams are especially collectible, with the oldest dating back to 1853.

- Last but not least, figure out where you're going to get your watch repaired. Old watches are especially capricious, but even new ones will need a loving tinkerer at some point. While there are plenty of websites, like TheWatchGuy.com, that advise you on how to fix your watch, problems you can't remedy by yourself may arise. It's also a little scary to mess around with super-old watches if you're not trained in the art of watch repair.

INTRODUCING W. W. POOL

BY JADE MILLER

The best thing about living in city as old as Richmond, Virginia, is the folklore that comes with it. Around Halloween, one's interest tends to shift to the spookier side of a city's history. Of course, Richmonders consider Poe and the Civil War old hat, but how about the Richmond Vampire?

The legend goes that on October 2, 1925, there was a huge tunnel cave-in in the Church Hill Tunnel on the Chesapeake and Ohio Railroads line. This collapse buried many men alive. Shortly after the cave-in, a figure emerged from the wreckage, covered in blood, the red and viscous fluid dripping from its jagged teeth. Strips of flesh hung from the creature's body, seemingly freshly removed from the men beneath the clay. This creature fled towards the James River and was tracked until it disappeared into the tomb of W. W. Poole, located in Hollywood Cemetery, more than twenty blocks away from the disaster site.

As fantastical as the story sounds, the Richmond Vampire's background as a man is really quite ordinary. Born in Mississippi, the second born of five sons, William Wortham Poole moved to Virginia in the 1860s and became a clerk in a tobacco factory in Manchester. From there, he worked as a private secretary as well as a bookkeeper and did the traditional thing of getting married and having children. He seemed to die unremarkably in 1913 at the age of eighty.

Yet, if this man was the Richmond Vampire, what interesting circumstances about his death have been kept under wraps? Who did he meet the night he died to go from aging bookkeeper to creepy creature of the night?

Unfortunately, not much has happened on the vampire front since the initial sighting in the early 1920s. All modern glimpses of this vampire, aside from the mysterious times the door to the mausoleum has been unlocked and left ajar, echo the original tale, leaving one to wonder if the vampire was really seen at all. The only worthwhile news was when Poole's bones decorated the hill behind his tomb in a Satanic symbol, prompting the big wigs at Hollywood Cemetery to place Poole's bones elsewhere. Their current location is a mystery.

Despite the yearnings of Quail Bell(e)s for things to go bump in the night, this vampire's reign is not as immortal as one would come to believe from vampire lore.

FAMOUS FOR FAIRY TALES

BY CHRISTINE STODDARD

Artists—perhaps more so than any other category of people— are painfully familiar with the hopelessness and despair that finds company with broken dreams. (And the fact that black clothing is good for hiding coffee stains.) Prone to developing grandiose illusions, artists often set unattainable goals, only to plummet into the angst of reality. Writer Hans Christian Andersen knew this free-fall hell quite well.

From childhood onward, he spent his days longing for a career in theater. Instead of playing with other kids, young Hans huddled up with a little puppet theater his father had built. He entertained neighbors with stories and songs. But Hans was a clunky child who grew into an even clunkier man.

Far taller and ganglier than most anyone he encountered, Hans was simply too awkward for the elegance of the nineteenth-century Danish stage. He also repeatedly proved to be a disappointing pupil and heartbroken lover. Over and over again, his friends and mentors tried to push him into an apprenticeship so he could support himself by learning a skilled trade. Hans retaliated each and every time, insisting that he was meant to be a great actor. Thus, more often than not, Hans subjected himself to pitiable living conditions, which he occasionally escaped thanks to others' kindness.

After many failed attempts to secure steady acting work, Hans turned to playwriting and eventually writing short stories. His inventive fairy tales gained him fame that persists around the world even today. If you grew up with "The Little Mermaid," "The Ugly Duckling," "The Princess and the Pea," "Thumbelina," "The Emperor's New Suit," or "The Snow Queen," you grew up with Hans Christian Andersen's brainchildren—or at least bastardized versions of them. During his lifetime, Hans published 168 fairy tales. In other words, his Plan C worked.

Fledglings, if you need some motivation after a few nasty hiccups, look at Hans. Pick up one of his fairy tales or check out a biography for the details of his early misery. In Hans' case, the answer to the fame he craved really did lie in fairy tales—the very things that had caused so many of his personal mishaps. His imagination was simply too big for other people's taste. That is, until he matched his imagination with discipline and got to writing what he was meant to write.

Maybe you can find a way to get your perception of truth and The Ultimate Truth to walk hand in hand like Hansie Boy did.

OLD SAN JUAN:
SPANISH HISTORY BUFFS UNITE!
BY LUNA LARK

I stumbled off the airplane in a stupor, hardly cognizant of the fact that I had arrived. The stink of plastic-wrapped blankets still clung to me. Despite my Herculean will, I could barely budge my eyelids or put one foot in front of the other without tripping. My makeup had somehow dribbled all over my face and every strand of my hair seemed to worship the ceiling. But I deserved little pity. My six-hour bus ride from Richmond, Virginia, to New York City and the subsequent two-hour flight had led me to the tropical and historical glory of San Juan, Puerto Rico. I was grateful for the escape, even if I was less than alert. Soon I would be visiting one of the oldest European settlements in the Americas.

A cloud of humidity and scores of singing frogs greeted me as I first encountered the island in darkness. Curse the color spots, I muttered. My vision had to adjust from the glaring institutional white I had abandoned a mere moment ago to the vast blackness beyond the line of taxis.

After some awkward negotiations with a middle-age taxi driver, I staggered into the hotel lobby and mumbled the necessary words to the receptionist. I plopped down before the computer humming a few feet away from the front desk. The desire to check my email suddenly possessed me. I sent a few messages to my most beloved explaining that I had yet to be kidnapped or enchanted by any Spanish Colonial architecture. Then, noting my growling stomach, I ran to the only nearby restaurant open at three A.M.—Burger King (whose menu differed drastically from the one I grew up with in the Mid-Atlantic United States.)

I was staying in the rather beachy El Condado, a district located near Old San Juan, the city's Colonial heart. Needless to say, as I'm a Quail Bell(e), Old San Juan was the district that most arrested my attention.

During my four days of mostly aimless (but happy) wandering, I discovered a historic district unlike any other I had ever seen. I grew up on the East Coast of the United States, where British Colonial villages abound. Particularly in my home state of Virginia, historic districts are practically commonplace.

In Richmond, where I currently live, there's The Fan, Shockoe Bottom, and Church Hill. Within a three hour drive, there's Old Town Fredericksburg, Old Town Leesburg, Old Town Winchester, Old Town Manassas, and, my favorite, Old Town Alexandria. There are also many other historical districts whose names do not begin with the words "Old Town"—take Jamestown, Staunton, and Charlottesville, for example.

My point is that blue cobblestones and Terra-cotta roofs by the sea are not the norm in any of these Virginian towns. Like a little girl, I marveled at such basic differences between British Colonial and Spanish Colonial. Yes, I had been to multiple historic cities over the years—from Edinburgh to La Rochelle to Old Montréal—but this was my first time in the Caribbean.

What first caught me in Old San Juan was the matter of shades and hues. You can't ignore the vibrant, pure colors. Imagine bright pinks and oranges, mostly variations of coral. You'll notice sunshine yellow, sky blue, and a range of other shocking shades, too. Well, at least "shocking" compared to the more conservative tones of Antebellum and Victorian era architecture. Even in The Fan, the largest Victorian and Edwardian architectural district in the United States and a place where homeowners tend to be more playful than in other parts of the Commonwealth, neutral colors abound. I put the architecture in Floridian terms since I have vacationed in the state almost every year since birth. Old San Juan seems to fuse the palette of Miami with the silhouettes of St. Augustine.

Another huge departure from what I knew back home was the matter of architectural materials. In Virginia, many of the historic buildings are made of brick or wood board. In Old San Juan, stucco and stone dominate. On this same note, gardens are not landscaped with magnolias and dogwoods. Instead, palm and banana trees make up the materials of San Juan gardens—gardens, mind you, that are located in lush courtyards, not on lavish lawns full of topiary.

The language, of course, isn't the same, either. All of the Old San Juan museum signs appear in Spanish first, English second, assuming they provide an English translation at all. As a hispanohablante, this did not bother me. In fact, it delights me. In Virginia, despite the large Hispanic population, many museum signs and brochures only appear in English. (Massively popular historic sites like Colonial Williamsburg aside.) In Old

San Juan, no one can claim there's a shortage of Spanish "Ye Olde" signs. For those who don't read Spanish, I hope it's a treat to admire the Colonial typography apparent in so many labels, plaques, and signs.

Something else that struck me about my visit is simply the historic vibe that emanates from Spanish conquerors versus English ones. I cannot articulate what it is, but I can assure that you, too, will feel it if you ever see Old San Juan. I just sensed very distinctive ghosts in Old San Juan. The burden of imperialism and slavery was there just as it is in any European settlement in America. Yet the ghosts talk differently, dress differently, and haunt differently from the ones who inhabit Virginia. I closed my eyes and thought of the men and women who walked here centuries ago. Colonial Spaniards, Indians . . . everyone roaming about half-purposefully, as if they were not quite aware that one day their most trivial actions would be recorded as history, whether political, economic, cultural, or social.

Clearly, smaller, subtler differences between the historic districts in Virginia and Old San Juan exist, but now I'd like to mention the must-sees in Old San Juan:

If you ever go to Old San Juan, definitely visit the two "castles": Fort San Felipe del Morro and San Juan de Cristóbal. Built in the 1500s, El Morro is a great stone citadel, while San Juan de Cristóbal, the biggest Spanish fortification built in the Americas, dates back to the seventeenth century and therefore looks slightly less ancient. Another fantastic site is the governor's mansion, El Palacio de Santa Catalina. Radiating a breezy blue with hints of white, El Palacio de Santa Catalina dates back to the 1500s. These are the district's three "biggies." If you're in Old San Juan for more than a quick two-hour cruise stop, check out any of the following: Santa María Magdalena de Pazzi, Museum of Ballajá, San José Church, Hotel El Convento, Casa Blanca, Cathedral of San Juan Bautista, and Paseo de la Princesa.

When I went home four days later, I felt privileged to have experienced such beautiful, historic splendor as exists in Old San Juan. Now if only I can get these conquistador phantoms to stop trailing me . . .

GETTIN' GORGEOUS THE REGENCY WAY

BY SANDRA SCHOLES

T hink of all the beauty products we have at our disposal these days, those professional makeup artists use and endorse, plus new, ingenious creams for keeping the modern woman looking younger despite the rigors of modern life. Back in the Regency era, beauty products were a little more basic and sometimes even dangerous to use. Just as we consider certain looks unfashionable, those of the Regency era had similar thoughts. They deemed freckles and heavy makeup unflattering. There were plenty of products available for those who did not wish to be regarded as unfashionable by polite society, but often ladies purchased raw ingredients and mixed them themselves.

Anti-Freckle Lotion

Since freckles were considered unattractive, ladies of the day used several products to temporarily bleach them. One such product was called Unction of Maintenon. It removed both light and dark colored freckles. Using Unction of Maintenon required covering the face completely with elderflower water at night and then applying unction oil. In the morning, the lady would cleanse her face with rose oil (or "oil of rose"). Below are steps to make Unction of Maintenon.

- Venice soap (1 ounce)
- Lemon juice (1/2 ounce)
- Bitter almond oil (1/4 ounce)
- Oil of tartar (1/4 ounce)
- Oil of rhodium (3 drops)

After adding the lemon juice and twin oils to the Venice soap, place the entirety in the sun until its consistency becomes water-like, only then adding the rhodium.

Make-up Tips

The emphasis on makeup during the Regency era was much subtler than it is today. The overall "painted" look was considered vulgar. Instead, they emphasized skin care over heavy makeup. Only the lips and cheeks were to show the merest hint of color. The face powder of the period was made of rice flour or talcum powder. White bismuth was used if a lady wanted a more pearlescent look.

- Cheeks: Pear's Liquid Blooms of Roses was one of the more popular ways to rouge the cheeks during the Regency period. There were several shades of carmine to choose from, all made from cochineal in alum water. Such things as tin were used in the making of this product and that was far from healthy, though the high quantities of the carmine were lessened if mixed with talcum powder.
- Eyes: Burnt cork and lamp black soot were mixed to provide a form of mascara and eyebrow cosmetic (a technique derived from the Egyptians and Turkish). The common drawback of using this tactic was its strong smell.
- Lips: Rose Lip Salve was the most used lip balm in Regency times, even when the use of color on the lips was considered slightly outrageous for a woman of means. It contained white wax, almond oil, and alkanet for color and rose oil to lend a pleasant smell. Vermillion was also a popular shade and was made from cochineal (this was also the closest in appearance to our lipsticks of today).

Day and Night Wash

Lastly, this is how women of the day commonly cleaned their faces, giving them that extra glow of beauty:

- Add lemon juice and spoonful of white brandy to a half pint of milk before boiling it.
- Scrape the scum from the surface, leaving it until cool.

It is amazing how much cosmetics and general beauty has changed over the years, yet if it hadn't been for early makeup, we might never have developed today's modern ways of making ourselves look that extra bit more beautiful than we already are.

TIP YOUR TOP HAT
TO THE TOP 10 VICTORIAN FILMS
BY MIRANDA SCHMIDT

T
he Victorian Age was an inarguably cinematic time. From bright and intricate dresses to stately top hats and horse-drawn carriages to ornate architecture, this was a time just begging to put in pictures. There are so many Victorian-centered movies that it's hard to choose just a few but I've done my best to choose a diverse top ten.

Wilde
With Stephen Fry playing the ever-witty and ultimately tragic Oscar Wilde, this movie already has a lot going for it. But cast Jude Law as Wilde's lover, the spoiled but beautiful Boise, and you really can't go wrong.

Moulin Rouge
Baz Luhrmann takes on late Victorian Paris in this most spectacular movie. Starring Nicole Kidman as a Parisian courtesan who longs to be an actress and Ewan McGregor as a young English writer in search of love and adventure, this film mixes romantic Victorian detail and contemporary pop culture to create a world uniquely its own.

The Age of Innocence
Martin Scorcese's film highlights the sexual repression in Edith Wharton's novel—who can forget Daniel Day-Lewis tremblingly caressing Michelle Pfeiffer's foot in a carriage? From the strangely pornographic-like blooming flower montage of the credits to the last shot of an old and regretful Day-Lewis walking out of frame amid flying pigeons, this film is a masterpiece of subtlety.

Dracula

Francis Ford Coppola's take on this Victorian tale captures the story's blood-curdling gothic horrors with a chilling perfection. Starring Winona Ryder and Gary Oldman at his most monstrous, sexy, and pitiable, this classic film explores Victorian repression, sex, violence, and the destructive powers of love.

Corpse Bride

Tim Burton's animated tale of a man's attempt to escape the corpse of a bride who has taken to him on the night before his wedding, this movie is stylish, fun, chilling, and very Burtonesque.

An Ideal Husband

Based on the play by Oscar Wilde, this hilariously satirical movie stars Cate Blanchett, Minnie Driver, Rupert Everett, Julianne Moore, and Jeremy Northam as members of the English aristocracy enmeshed in the social mores and societal expectations of their class and era.

Topsy-Turvy

A hilarious rendering of Gilbert and Sullivan's creation of *The Mikado*, directed by Mike Leigh and starring Jim Broadbent and Allan Corduner, this movie full of music and mishap was nominated for a number of British Academy of Film and Television Arts (BAFTA) awards (including "Best Picture") and is certainly not to be missed by the Victorian enthusiast.

The French Lieutenant's Woman

Starring Meryl Streep and Jeremy Irons as actor/lovers, this film based off of John Fowles' same-titled novel explores the dividing line between the imagined and the real as it bops back and forth between scenes from the Victorian movie and contemporary scenes showing the making of it. Oddly enough, in the end, the Victorian "movie" sections seem far more real than the contemporary "real" ones.

Being Julia

Annette Bening plays a famous Victorian actress beginning to feel her age. It's a great film, most notable for Bening's portrayal of this domineering, stage-y, eccentric and, ultimately, fragile woman.

Far and Away

Set in Ireland and America, this Ron Howard movie follows the exploits of two young Irish people, one from the Anglo-Irish landowning class (played by Nicole Kidman) and one poor land worker who is about to be evicted (played by Tom Cruise). The two set out for an American adventure that charts the course of Irish immigration and ends with the Oklahoma Land Run of 1893.

MAY I SEE YOUR PEEPERS, MADAM?

BY JADE MILLER

As every Quail Bell(e) knows, the field of beauty products is constantly changing, updating, and modernizing its merchandise to capitalize on the newest trends and latest looks. However, one staple in every girl's vanity stand defies that standard and truly embodies the saying "If it isn't broken, don't fix it."

In its most basic form, an eyelash curler is a beauty tool with a rubber strip between two pieces of metal that is applied to the upper eyelashes and squeezed in order to crimp and curl the lashes. The eyelash curler was patented April 7, 1931, and the images drawn in the patent application look very much the same as the eyelash curlers seen on the market today. Originally called Rodal, the brand smartly changed the product's name to Kurlash.

In today's modern society, the eyelash curler generally appears as a beauty staple on fashion shows like *Project Runway* or *RuPaul's Drag Race* as well as on sitcoms, like in the intro for the pilot of *Whitney*. To the men who produce television shows, the eyelash curler seems to represent the lengths a woman will go to in order to make herself beautiful.

However, the eyelash curler is really just a simple tool, a cog in the beauty machine, essentially the same as a razor is to a man. The debate in most beauty blogs now is not if a woman should use one but which brand should gain her loyalty. Shu Uemura and Shiseido, two companies that have basically the same product, are at the center of the debate. Which one a woman chooses comes down to personal preference (and perhaps price) as well as how she curls her lashes.

The Shiseido is lighter than the Shu, which can have an effect on how hard someone curls the lashes by overcompensating for the heavy weight, giving a heavier crimp as opposed to a gentler squeeze. The Shu is a bit wider than the Shiseido and thus can result in pinching to get to those lashes on the very ends of the lids, which can hurt on the sensitive skin of the eyelid. Still, the Shu and the Shiseido both give a good curl, but if a longer lasting curl is the aim, the Shu is the way to go.

A multitude of differences stand between being a woman in the 1930s and being a woman in the 2010s. In a constantly changing world where things can be worrisome or uncertain, it is good to know that some things always stay the same.

VICTORIAN GOTHIC
CASTLE ON THE JAMES RIVER

BY JOSEPHINE STONE

E legance and utility come together in Richmond's very own castle on the river, where Richmonders can take a step, or minuet, rather, back in history to where water once pumped under dancing feet.

Among myriad projects fronted by the mostly single-man show that is the James River Park System, one of the latest in the works is the restoration of the historic pump house that sits on the periphery of Byrd Park near Dogwood Dell and the Nickel Bridge. The man with the plan and director of the park system, Ralph White, paints a beautiful picture of what is to come if all goes according to plan.

"My dream is to have tiki torches. You'll have a glass of wine and go by electric motorboat that looks like an old bateau . . . You go up the river and come back," White says as he waves his arm over the wooden railing of the ramp to the pump house toward the water.

The experience White wants to provide with the pump house is of a more mature nature, making the park very different from the others that line the James. Most cater to the younger, more athletic crowd, and, by making the pump house a place for nostalgic social gatherings, those interested in less active activities can come together.

"Imagine this. You come here for coffee. Then you walk up the hill to catch a show at Dogwood Dell," White says smiling. "And then you come back and go for a boat ride."

Historic tourism, White mentions, is something that does not need to be traveled far for.

"People go to Europe all the time to look at old castles and they don't expect them to be modern structures . . . and this is our old castle," White says of the Victorian Gothic structure.

Getting Richmond's old castle to function in a friendly manner will take some work, such as minor construction completed largely by volunteers and the addition of a water fountain and bathroom to get the building up to regulation. After that, hopefully, the rest will be history . . . or more like walking, drinking, and dancing in a piece of history.

The pump house, in its heyday, was the pumping station that supplied all of the drinking water for the city of Richmond and was the second one ever constructed. The impact of the pump house was great. Where fires would once turn residential blocks to ash in a matter of minutes, now there was a hydrant system in play that greatly affected the insurance rates and safety of the city.

Lyn Lanier, the Saturday morning tour guide whom White describes as a "depository of knowledge of [pump house] history," has been working in the pump house park for twelve years. According to Lanier, the original water pumps installed in the house were too weak, and steam power was soon utilized.

They went up to Philadelphia to the exposition there . . . and they saw the steam pump on display. They bought it, brought it back, and it installed in forty-two days," Lanier says. "The building, however, was decommissioned in 1924."

Before and after the decommission of the pump house as a pump house, though, the building always emphasized public use. Colonel Cutshaw, war hero and architect, designed the building so that it could have double use—as a place for function and for entertainment (hence the sophisticated design of the building). This public utility was as literal as that.

"The public walkway is where the public could view their utility," White says, pointing toward the ceiling in the pump room. The tour of the pump house leads from the furnace room to the main pump room, the building possessing a layout like "layers of an onion," White says. But it is in this room where things get interesting and where the emphasis on elegance begins.

The room was "designed for the public to view in awe of what the government is providing its citizens," White says. "People were invited to come and ladies would dress to the nines with their long, flowing skirts and their whalebone corsets and their little parasols. They'd come by in boats in order to see the pumps."

This is where White's imagination is again taken to the future in an attempt to tie in the sentimental history with a modern use of the building.

"Now imagine the entire ledge lit with candles, floating candles in the water, and either a radio or a legitimate guitarist or flutist in the corner . . .

sounds echoing off the stone walls along with the dripping water," White says poetically.

"Wouldn't this be a cool place for a cocktail party?" A smile breaks across his wistful face as he describes the pump house's future.

Now on to the center and final layer of the onion that is the pump house—the dance floor. A brief walk up a flight of stairs above the utility is a place for the public to cut the rug in a forty-foot wide, eighty-foot long open-air room overlooking the river.

According to White, in the 1880s and 1890s, Richmond's upper-crust would don their ball gowns, the women in their bustiers and faux beauty marks, the men in their cuffs and lace. The dance of the time, the minuet, was an imitation of the aristocratic European dance.

"They came for elegant things . . . and then in the late 1890s, the trolley system was extended to here and that changed everything," White says. "Ain't no woman in the world gonna get onto the trolley with a bustier and a big hoop skirt, so the clientele changed and it stopped being the richest of the rich."

With the turn of the century and with newly created accessibility for the middle class to the dance hall, there was a call for practicality over elegance. In 1905, additions were built to both ends of the hall, and a back wall was created to block the rain and wind, natural elements that had been normal hindrances of the hall. Out was the original design created by Colonel Cutshaw that embodied the forests of Europe with elaborate lancet arches, bare stone, and wood in grays and browns. In were walls for the weather and colored glass.

"This is king's dominion. This isn't elegant anymore. This is now middle class. It's functional, realistic, and you know what, you control access, weather, and you have brilliant colors," White says of the wall with glass panes in raspberry, gold, and red.

Other American milestones, such as the days of speakeasies and World War II, added to the slow digression of the pump house dance hall clientele. In the '30s, speakeasies popped up along the road toward the pump house, where, according to White, men could get a shot of "Dutch courage before trying out their two left feet dancing."

During the war, women's dance partners were sent abroad and, as quickly as the elegance sashayed out of the building, the days of the dance hall were done. To keep the economy with the momentum of war production, energies shifted toward the production of automobiles and soon most people in the city had one. This is where, White says, the need for a public dance space took a back seat.

"The reason for a dance floor was to have a legitimate place where a respectable woman could come to meet a man and touch. Where you could hug, whisper . . . where you could court . . . All in the safety of the public," White says. "But with the advent of the automobile, there were back seats and privacy and there was no more need for dance floors."

In 1952, the last public dance was hosted and the pump house was then abandoned to gracefully deteriorate. Weather beaten with a saggy roof and fixtures stolen for scrap dealing, the pump house was adopted by the James River Park System in the late 1980s, around when White began his lifelong venture to preserve the natural and historical assets of Richmond.

With the help of Lanier, Bill Trout, Chris Newcomb, and various volunteers, the major repairs, such as the stabilization of the floor and roof—what White says is "the stuff of legends"—were done, to the chagrin of the local government, without contractors. The unconventional repairs made by the park system with virtually no funding actually worked, and now White's dreams are even closer to realization.

"That's the story of the salvation of this building and of the future for opening it up for public use. Then bring on the cocktail parties, weddings, bar mitzvahs . . . " White says.

White says that October is the best time to come see the pump house, the "glory days" so to speak, in which you can see the building surrounded by golden leaves. With the light slanting in just right, Richmond's castle is beautifully illuminated. Since this article was published, White has retired.

WISE WORDS FOR VISITING A VICTORIAN BROTHEL

BY SIR GEARHEART

I t is the mid to late 1800s in the hustling, bustling city of London. Carriages and parasols abound. You are a handsome, well-to-do gentleman who dresses fashionably (however, no one could reasonably call you a dandy). You make more than a decent living and are proud of your place in the minor aristocracy.

About three years ago, you married a beautiful young lady prone to blushing. Love-making stupefies her, not out of pure pleasure but rather pure fear. She considers sex her duty as a wife who must produce a healthy heir to your estate. That she might enjoy the act has never once entered her pretty head. Instead, she finds it painful, vulgar, and dull. Lying back, she thinks of England, just as Queen Victoria instructed her daughter on her wedding night.

You hate the way your wife grits her teeth and cries softly in the bedroom, curls plastered to the pillow like an anguished lamb moments before slaughter. If only she learned to like it—and you and your touch and your sweat. But given her stern upbringing and current social mores, that shall never happen. She must find more wholesome sources of amusement, whether in sewing or reading or singing. In lacing her corset, she will never hold her body sacred, only shameful. Anything you say to compliment her figure will simply disgust her.

You, on the other hand, can no longer ignore your sexual desires. A Victorian man must pursue his conquests.

That is why you stepped into this bawd-house. You have remained faithful to your wife up until this point but refuse to lead a life of dissatisfaction for yet another day. Your cousin, who experienced similar trifles, recommended this very establishment. To calm yourself during your first couple minutes on the premises, you remember the words of wisdom he uttered:

- Do not bring drink or other drugs to the brothel, lest you wish to be dismissed as soon as you come.

- The women in this establishment shall dress unlike any female creature you've ever seen. They do not wear bonnets or shawls and prefer gaudy, clingy fabrics—precisely why we call them laced muttons.

- Unlike ladies, prostitutes shall not shy beneath your stare. So stare on! Lord knows your wife will never let you admire her bubbies, muff, and blind cupid.

- Language that would normally shock your wife never bothers a prostitute. Feel free to wag your tongue with talk of twiddle-diddles, quail-pipes, lay-cocks, plug-tails, kettledrums, and prigging. If you become particularly skilled at wielding raunchy words, the Madam of the house might, out of appreciation, lend you her toffer (that is, the best prostitute on call).

- Be prepared to pay more to bed a virgin, as they are less likely to be disease-ridden. But beware! Do not confuse a menstruating whore for a maiden. These "fallen women" have their tricks, just like any other merchant.

- Should you acquire a venereal disease, having sex with a child shall cure your ailment. As children cost dearly, try to inspect prostitutes for sores and rashes before accepting their services. (Some women attempt to hide their afflictions with merkins.) Remember that prevention is better than cure.

- You may find yourself habitually seeing the same prostitute. Depending on just how often you see her, taking her on as your mistress may be the most prudent option. Put her up in a row house and provide her with an ample stipend.

- If you tire of the brothel I have recommended, try one of the many others in the city or simply fetch a streetwalker out of the gutter. There are, in fact, at least 20,000 of these amorous nymphs in London alone. You may read some of their biographies and descriptions of their sexual offerings in any number of gentleman's publications.

ONE WAY TO PROPERLY REMEMBER A PET

BY JULIE DINISIO

Your beloved cat, dog, rabbit, bird, lizard, rodent, or other such pet has passed on to . . . wherever pets go when they die. Now what? Most pet owners probably aren't thinking in advance about what they will do with the body of their pet when tragedy befalls.

If the pet dies at home, many people simply bury it in the backyard, which can be legal or illegal depending on the locale. If the pet dies at the vet's office, the owner often relinquishes the body to be properly disposed of, usually by means of cremation. However, there is a third, somewhat popular option—burial in a pet cemetery.

Faithful Friends Pet Cemetery, in conjunction with Washington Memorial Park (a human cemetery), is located in Sandston, Virginia, and offers all the services possibly needed to bury a beloved animal. Faithful Friends has been in existence since 1949, when Washington Memorial Park came into being. It is currently managed by Matthew Canfield who said, in reference to the animal end of the business, "We are a funeral home for pets."

Canfield estimated the cost of the average pet burial at about $1,500, though it ultimately depends on the size of the deceased. This amount includes keeping the animal in cold storage if necessary and providing a proper, sealable casket. No chemicals are put into the pets' bodies. Memorial plaques and services are available at an extra cost. According to Canfield, a pastor is always on hand for humans and pets, and many former owners will play music and adorn the grave with flowers during the service.

"The services can be very emotional, probably just as emotional at a pet funeral as at a person funeral," attests Canfield.

Anything involving the Rainbow Bridge is bound to be after all, or so he says. Upon my inquiry as to what the Rainbow Bridge is, he informed me of this resting place for loved pets. When the owner dies, he/she and the pet will eventually meet up in joyous reunion on the bridge.

Faithful Friends Pet Cemetery is home to a couple hundred pets, and roughly twenty more are buried each year. According to Canfield, the pet burial business has not suffered from the slow economy, and why would it? Not many people are going to spend thousands of dollars to bury their dog or cat, good or bad economy. For those who do, though, it is a memorable—albeit sentimental—way to properly remember one of your best friends.

GETTING SOMETHING TO CINCH THAT WAIST

BY JADE MILLER

When looking into buying a corset, browsing the World Wide Web makes you feel like you're on a quest for the Holy Grail. Quail Bell's here to give you some boning behind this garment.

First of all, you as the buyer need to decide if you would like an actual corset or a corset-style top. The difference is all in the boning, as a corset is boned with steel and shapes a woman's body by redistributing the body's fat to create a more voluptuous shape. A corset-style top (or bustier) is boned with plastic and is only a fashion piece with no real shaping. Do not wear a bustier as an actual corset—that can hurt you and perpetuates the rumors that corsets are bad for you. A properly fitted corset should not hurt, and if anything, does very minimal damage to the body.

Now that that's straightened out, let's move on to the more interesting tidbits that come with buying a corset. The number one thing to keep in mind is that corsets, true and well-made corsets, don't come cheap. A corset can range in price from $100 to $1000. However, the saying that "you get what you pay for" certainly applies here, as making a corset takes time and serious skill. So be wary of Etsy.com and eBay.com sellers who offer corsets for $50 (it's probably a bustier).

You have many choices to make before buying your corset. First off, do you want off-the-rack or custom made? Obviously, custom made is the best way to go, as those corsets are made to your exact measurements and, really, if you have a more shapely body, this is probably the smarter way to go. If you have a pretty standard size body, then off-the-rack will work just fine and is naturally the slightly cheaper route. When sizing, the rule of thumb is two to four inches smaller than your natural waist. So, a 30" waist becomes a 26" with bust and hips, and almost every corset is sized by the waist, so really stick with that measurement. Some women will be able to cinch in 6" or even more. This all depends on your body and your comfort.

Then, of course, there's the underbust corset, which starts at the ribs and ends at the hips, or the overbust option, which covers the breasts. There are also modesty panels, different types of grommets and steel, and decorations like lace and ribbons.

The best thing to do when looking for a corset is to get out there and research! Only go with vendors who are trustworthy and have great reviews, since there is a lot of money involved and a long time between pay and getting your finished product. And always, always get dates for when to expect your piece.

Once you get your corset, there's not much you can't do in them, but try to lace up loosely before eating or drinking to keep from cramping. Also keep in mind the little things like going to the bathroom and putting on your shoes—the corset will present slight challenges in the beginning.

A Quail Bell(e) is always the epitome of vintage fashion, and it wouldn't do to have an unlaced Victorian-style Oxford when every other piece of your outfit is perfection!

MELANCHOLIC LANDMARK IN CITY'S EPICENTER

BY JOSEPHINE STONE

I had never been to Cincinnati until Labor Day weekend 2011 because I'd previously never had a reason to go. I am sure "Visiting all fifty states" lies somewhere mid-way down my bucket list, but I am also sure that Ohio was not toward the top of those fifty. A friend's wedding sent my husband and me with a RideShare friend-of-a-friend driving ten hours northwest of Richmond. We frequented rest stops, ate fried food, and rotated turns picking albums on the iPod.

What is there to see in Cincinnati, the home of the Reds, the Bengals, and Skyline chili? With minimal knowledge and expectations of our destination, this long-distance river city was a blank canvas in our minds. It was clear, however, after riding our exit ramp past the illuminated skyline, that this trip would not disappoint.

Most aspects of the city were similar to other large cities—towering buildings, hundreds of people out and about, an art district, neighborhoods in boroughs, and glorious public transit. But there was something dark about this city that we wouldn't discover until later.

Taking the number three bus straight to the thriving center of the business district, we found ourselves at Fountain Square—a large, outdoor area complete with tables and chairs, a performance stage, and, you guessed it, a fountain in the center of it all. This is where the beautiful morbidity comes into the picture.

The Tyler Davidson Fountain is located at 5th and Vine Streets, and analyzing it from an emotional, uninformed interpretation of this piece of art, it is the saddest and most sexual fountain I have ever seen. A young woman stands above everyone, showering water on the relief carvings and statues below. The only thing is that her hands do not look giving. Her hands are downturned nonchalantly as the peasant women and children below her fight to fill their vases. Nothing about this woman conveys wholesome fertility. In the middle of Cincinnati, there's a struggle between a beautiful woman with everything, standing above those who need her to live.

Surrounding the fountain are several naked young men, each straddling a different animal, a snake, turtle, or fish. Water pours from each animal's mouth into a basin below. The symbolism is obvious.

Fountain Square is the place to be on a midsummer's afternoon, with people of all ages gathered around at tables and perched along the edge of the Tyler Davidson. As I sat, slowly moving my hand back and forth in the clear water full of coins, I wondered to myself if anyone else saw the sadness in the woman watching over Cincinnati.

SHADING THE NAUGHTY BITS

BY PAISLEY HIBOU

I t's a given. One of the most unnecessarily awkward conversations you will have in your life takes place between the ages of twelve and sixteen. This sweat-inducing, one-way talk will occur on an unassuming afternoon or early evening. You will have just cleaned your plate of that last liver slab and have but one question on your mind: Where does Mom keep the extra minty toothpaste?

But approximately 0.03 seconds after you've excused yourself from the table, Dad will clear his throat and start fidgeting with his sleeves. Mom will motion toward Dad. That's when your father, normally a harmless, likeable fellow, will say, "Your mother and I want to talk to you." Did they know you lied about finishing your chemistry homework? No. But they do know you've been wildly misinformed about The Birds and the Bees—and they're about to bash every sex myth you ever learned in the schoolyard.

After Mom and Dad's polite, clinical explanations, you will flee to your room, ashamed yet still curious. There are two questions they failed to answer: 1) What the hell is a pastie?, and 2) What the hell is a merkin?

Yet these are not questions any sane person asks his mother or father. These questions are best asked of bored, slightly perverted magazine writers. Thus, though it has been many a year since your bar mitzvah or quinceañera, you will at long last learn the truth about pasties and merkins.

Pasties are adhesive nipple covers often used in burlesque dancing, stripping, and other forms of sensual or erotic entertainment. They popped up in the 1920s to prevent dancers from breaking anti-toplessness laws. Generally speaking, pasties are just large enough to cover the breast's areola. Like any article of clothing, pasties come in various styles, depending upon the designer's preference. Sometimes pasties have tassels. Sometimes they have sequins. Sometimes they have tassels AND sequins.

Somewhere out there floating in the universe are pasties with googly eyes and fishtails. Pasties are, after all, primarily tricks of the showgirl trade.

Pasties do have a place offstage, though. Women of all kinds of "reputations" wear pasties under backless dresses and even T-shirts (especially sheer ones). Think of them as nipple shades. These tamer versions of pasties usually come in neutral colors like white or beige. Like a Band-Aid, you simply remove the layer of waxy paper on the back to reveal a thin layer of adhesive. Then you place the adhesive over your nipple and gently press the front side of the pastie. An instant later, bye-bye headlights! There's also such thing as pastie glue, though it's less appealing to the Average Jane. It's meant more often for higher-end, decorative pasties.

Anyone can buy pasties—and they don't need to prove they're eighteen, either. Bland ones are available most anyplace that sells bras, whether a department store or a lingerie boutique. Flashier ones are less readily available, though they're hardly rare finds. Many artists and designers sell pasties in their Etsy.com stores, for instance.

Etsy is an online compendium of boutiques from around the world. Most vendors display goods they handmade themselves. Fashion accessories, especially in the "alternative" vein, definitely dominate. Pasties, subsequently, run rampant.

As of September 18, 2011, Etsy vendor Hexotica of Melbourne, Australia, was toting cheery cupcake pasties in pink satin and lace. These foam "dessert boobies," as she described them, featured pink satin ribbon "frosting" and a lace/sequin "cup." Hexotica advertised that she offers a white version, as well as customizations. A tiny sampling of other Etsy vendors selling pasties include Goth Fox Designs, Estro Jenn's Designs, and VOLAC Designs. An Etsy search for the term "pasties" on September 24, 2011 revealed 1,462 results!

So now you have a little background on what the hoot pasties are. But what about what's down below?

Introducing . . . the merkin!

Merkins are pubic wigs that were originally employed by prostitutes and other promiscuous folks to conceal signs of STDs. Whether you had sores, rashes, or bald spots, your lover never had to know—as long as you got busy in the dark or with the presence of a few petticoats. Merkins have graced genitalia since at least the early 1600s. In the 1700s, merkins were often as ornate as head wigs with ribbon, cloth flowers, and other Rococo-like details.

Don't assume merkins are relics of the past, however. Now certain screen stars use them to escape the good girl's no-no of full-frontal nudity or to give a character's appearance more historical accuracy.

For an example of the latter case, take Kate Winslet in *The Reader*. Since the story takes place in 1958, Winslet could not have gotten away with showing her more modern grooming. Landing strips and Brazilian waxes, though common in the Generation X/Y world, barely existed in bygone days.

Merkins, with their old-timey kitschy reputation, can also bring humor to a movie scene. Take, for example, Heidi Klum's huge, red, fluffy merkin in *Blow Dry*. In *Harold & Kumar Escape from Guantanamo Bay*, several extras wore snow cone-esque merkins in red, white, and blue.

Merkins, given the West's current obsession with hair removal, don't have the same razzle-dazzle appeal of pasties. More often they're seen as funny, not sexy. That's why if you search for merkins on Etsy.com, only a couple dozen items appear. None of them are actual merkins, either. They're just novelty items poking fun at merkins. Nonetheless, certain sex shops, especially ones specializing in LGBTQ merchandise, do carry merkins. Some drag queens, for instance, like to wear merkins in order to cover their male genitalia.

Since certain regions still prevent strippers from dancing completely nude, they may wear merkins over flesh-colored panties to indulge customers. If the regional laws disallow toplessness, strippers likely wear pasties, too. As long as customers don't look too closely, they won't notice what UrbanDictionary.com calls "a toupee for the pubic area" and "nipple patches."

Imagine—merkins and pasties working in harmony both in the distant past and not-so-far future. It's a beautiful but strange planet we inhabit.

GREETINGS, FOLKLORE

BY BRAINY BIRD ———————————————

Her name is Folklore and she is the spirit of a society. She hovers over a people's traditions, melting into the music, steaming from the food, and pulsating in the words that storytellers wield to carve out their cultural insights. Like a placenta, Folklore enters the world from the birth canal and, like a skeleton, she exits the world in graves and ashes. Then she repeats the cycle one-thousand times a day in a thousand different locations. She inhabits North, South, East, and West; urban, rural, and suburban; yesterday, today, and tomorrow, too.

Folklore lingers in the corners of living rooms. She jumps out from books and slithers through films. If you watch closely—or at least manage to open your eyes for a moment—you'll spot Folklore on Christmas morning or at bedtime as you read your child tales you only thought you had forgotten.

Once, on my way home from school, I met Folklore. As I rounded a corner from one side and she from another, we bumped into each other. She felt soothingly plush, though I pretended not to notice her body. Given her multiple manifestations, I did not recognize her at first. I only asked who she was when I felt her staring at me. I mustered a fake cough and then asked if I knew her.

She replied, "You have known me all your life and, depending on how you regard me, will know me in death as well."

I paused, nodded, and bid her farewell, only to sight her a second later, coming at me from another direction.

There is no escaping the ubiquitous Folklore. This ghost haunts our dreams, memories, and precious random thoughts.

THE MAGIC
OF GORELORE

BY STARLING ROOT

Tim Burton is to cinema what Edgar Allen Poe is to literature: a master of the dark, bizarre, and mysterious. Burton's ghostly taste and "Goth" niche in Hollywood are undeniable. Films he has directed and/or produced include: *Sweeney Todd: The Demon Barber of Fleet Street, James and the Giant Peach, Batman Forever, The Nightmare Before Christmas,* and *Big Fish,* among many others. His influences range from Ray Harryhausen's animation to early Disney cartoons to Fellini to Vincent Price and more (Cortez 2004). Burton's films usually feature sinister palettes, deep shadows, the topics of love and belonging, and pariahs for principal characters. In order to convey his trademark themes and achieve his unique aesthetic, Burton employs a variety of special techniques. His use of stop-motion animation, elaborate makeup, dramatic lighting, and coloring truly distinguish his films from others made during our age of CGI omnipresence. For Burton, worshipping detail trumps all else.

In a time when most animators deem stop-motion animation and puppet films "a dying art," Burton continues using these techniques because they give the audience the feeling of actually "being there" (Burton 2008). Stop-motion animation is, according to some filmmakers, one of the most tedious forms of animation because it requires the progressive movement of an object between frames every 1/24 of a second (Burton 2008). In her 2001 article, "When Art Comes to Life," Amy Porter describes stop-motion animation as a "simple technology" possessing "nostalgic awkwardness" (12). Burton did not direct his most explicit stop-motion projects, like *Nightmare* and *Corpse Bride* in order to remove himself from the "painstakingly slow process" involved (Salisbury 71).

Burton's most famous stop-motion film is *The Nightmare Before Christmas*

(1993), directed by Henry Selick. Claymation, one of the most popularly known forms of stop-motion, entails the majority of the film's special effects. TV specials like *Rudolph the Red-Nosed Reindeer* and *How the Grinch Stole Christmas* inspired Burton in realizing his poem "The Nightmare Before Christmas" in film form. His illustrations drew upon the drawings of artists like Ronald Searle and Edward Gorey; Selick's crew then referred to Burton's illustrations for 3-D character and set design.

The crew, which consisted of 200 workers, even spread clay and plaster across the set and scratched it so it created the look of pen-and-ink cross-hatching. According to Selick, the film's production design resembled a "living illustration" (Burton 2008). Three to four people built all the *Nightmare* characters in oil-based clay over hand-machined ball and socket armatures. The puppets then had to be molded, injected with a foam latex material, and baked in an oven. Once removed from the oven, the characters' molding was peeled off and they were sent to the fabrication department.

In the fabrication department, artists attached clothing, hair, fur, and other finishing touches to the puppets; every detail counted, especially for close-up shots. Major characters, like Jack the Pumpkin King and Sally, required additional considerations, including a range of complex facial expressions. The team created hundreds of hand-sculpted replacement heads for Jack, allowing him to display a spectrum of emotions. Similarly, Sally wore interchangeable face masks so animators could manipulate her expressions. They decided against a full head change like Jack's to lessen the chance of animators accidentally ruining her long, red hair (Burton 2008).

Animators could not be assigned their own character(s); instead, all participants had to work as a group and took turns animating characters according to their personal strengths. As an example, certain animators were better at adjusting the puppets for close-up scenes while others' talents lied in creating very active motion.

Due to the slowness inherent to stop-motion animation, *Nightmare* required almost three years to finish. Every $\frac{1}{24}^{th}$ of a second required a new, only slightly different puppet pose. Consequently, crew members on average created a mere sixty seconds of film every week.

Burton's *Corpse Bride* (2005) relies heavily upon stop-motion animation techniques, as well. In fact, *Corpse Bride* employs much of the same techniques as *Nightmare*, relying heavily upon custom-made puppets moving across handmade sets. Differences between the two exist, however. In order to monitor the action of the puppets and ensure sleek movement, the crew shot the entire process digitally as opposed to using film as they did in

Nightmare. This allowed the animators to review individual frames as well as the overall flow of the project quickly and easily. *Corpse Bride* also depended upon a small amount of CGI, whereas *Nightmare* used exclusively claymation and small bits of second-layering traditional animation.

Beetlejuice (1988) ranks third as the Tim Burton film with the most stop-motion animation, employing the method for Hell scenes. *Pee-Wee Herman's Big Adventure* (1985), the first feature film that Burton directed, also makes use of stop-motion but to a far lesser extent than the aforementioned films because it is almost entirely live-action. Burton hired Rick Heinrichs, one of his CalArts classmates, for the stop-motion animation scenes (Salisbury 49). *James and the Giant Peach* (1996) features both stop-motion and live-action sequences, but it is primarily an animated film. Other Burton films that evidence stop-motion animation include: *Vincent* (1982) and *Frankenweenie* (1984).

Though stop-motion is extremely time-consuming and much more expensive than standard computer-generated imagery, Burton insists on applying the proper medium to the proper story. In an interview with Cinematical, he stated, ". . . You just do a project . . . in the medium that fits it and do a good story . . . It will connect if it's the right thing" (Gilchrist 2009).

Color is another huge element in Burton's films, created by careful lighting and, in the case of his puppet films, thoughtful hand-painting. On the miniature puppet sets of *Nightmare,* the crew used as many as twenty to thirty lights to steepen contrast and elongate shadows (Burton 2008). That represents as many lights as might be used on a live-action Hollywood set, showing that the crew applied large-scale film principles to an elaborate small-scale situation. Besides granting *Nightmare* a Gothic flair, the lights and colors contribute to the film's symbolism. In Halloween Land, everything appears in gloomy shades because the characters there lack the sincerity, hope, and imagination of a warmer atmosphere. In Christmas Land, the landscape buzzes with all the festive colors traditionally associated with the holidays; the waves of red, green, and gold allude to cheer and optimism. The Real World, where Jack goes to deliver presents, though, is much blander; the houses, the cars, the people—everything is a neutral tone or a humdrum pastel. In other words, reality hovers somewhere between Halloween Land and Christmas Land in terms of faith and rosy sentiments. Crew members in the fabrication department hand-painted everything on the Halloween Land, Christmas Land, and Real World sets.

Just as the color palette is very precise in *Nightmare* (with all its carefully chosen shades), *Corpse Bride* also features two main color families that help contrast two worlds through the use of diligent lighting and hand-painting. Life scenes show everything in grays, like tintypes, while Death scenes are much more flamboyant (Burton 2008). The life scenes therefore come across as uptight and dreary, whereas the death scenes read as significantly more relaxed and fun. Such a contrast also exists in *Edward Scissorhands*. Black, white, and gray prevail in Edward's isolated castle, which is one of the reasons why he looks so amiss in the suburbs, where tacky pastels prevail. Edward's castle is a place of loneliness and old-fashioned taste; the suburbs scream of neighborly attention and gaudiness.

Another effect essential to Tim Burton films is strange and enchanting makeup. Stan Winston is the man responsible for realizing many of Burton's monsters. For instance, he brought to life Burton's vision of Edward's glinting hands in *Edward Scissorhands* and Penguin's beak in *Batman Returns*. In the book, *Men, Makeup, and Monsters: Hollywood Masters of Illusion and Fx*, Winston explains that Edward's hands were basically gloves with seven blades attached to each hand (Timpone 48). In order to make Danny DeVito's penguin beak in *Batman Returns*, Winston created a single-piece prosthetic that extended from DeVito's forehead to his upper lip; afterwards, Winston smeared Tuttle rubber, greasepaint, and Par paint over the beak. Nappy hair extensions, decaying dentures, and Greg Cannom's three-finger appliances completed the overall villainous look (Timpone 52).

Beetlejuice is another example of a Burton film that employs impressive makeup effects, mostly in the realm of monster prosthetics. Robert Short, who won an Oscar for his work, oversaw all the makeup, including the creature effects that contributed to what the book *Ghosts and Angels in Hollywood Film: Plots, Critiques, Casts and Credits* calls "a banquet of wonderfully grotesque sights" (Parish 20).

Since the mid-1980s, Burton has forged his own niche with his spooky and fantastical cinematic visions. He draws upon a variety of esoteric influences and repeatedly explores the same themes. The question, then, is how exactly will he leave a mark on cinematic history? How will his pioneering into color/lighting, makeup, and stop-motion effects impact future dark-minded filmmakers? Whatever the answer may be, it is clear that Tim Burton's reputation for "gorelore" will persist throughout the rest of his career.

PITTSBURGH'S
'CREATIVE URBANIST'
BY CHRISTINE STODDARD

I first met Connor Sites-Bowen at The Cyberpunk Apocalypse Writers' Project one evening in January. The event was the cooperative's monthly Cool-Off, a sort of show-and-tell for artists, writers, and community artists in Pittsburgh. Connor and I immediately started chatting. Soon, I found him to be an engaging and curious fellow. A graduate of Carnegie Mellon University and an AmeriCorps food bank worker, Connor fell in love with Pittsburgh early on in his college career and wants nothing more than to nurture and explore the city. His recent project—a form of combined urban and environmental art—highlights his unique gift for seeing potential in a post-industrial city.

Who are you and what do you do? You may, of course, identify yourself with your superhero name.

Connor Sites-Bowen, Creative Urbanist and general appreciator of the weird, the strange, and the forgotten.

Tell me about your highly imaginative/pseudo science fiction project! It's about mushrooms and urban decay. What's it called?

Strangely enough, they don't really have a name. They are less a specific, targeted, nameable piece, and more like This Thing I Do. What This Thing I Do is, physically, is a series of paintings of figures, generally fungal, in black tempera on cardboard which I install, or give out to others to install, for me in decaying buildings around Pittsburgh that I wish to see digested and revived.

So, why mushrooms? Why not . . . worms, for instance?

Mushrooms and other fungi do this amazing thing when they need food. They emit or secrete enzymes into their environment that take the material around them and begin to break it down. They keep doing this until the material is, effectively, one step from being mushroom-flesh, at which point the fungal mass emits thousands or millions of cell-tentacles called mycelium which surround and encase the nutritious material, and quickly turn it into more fungal growth. It is only when their environment becomes too harsh and there is nothing left to break down and consume that fungi send tentacles of mycelium up to the surface, where they produce what we think of as "mushrooms"—many of which are poison-laced, so as to, hopefully, kill the creatures that eat them and produce more organic material to digest. Once a fungus has run its course, it leaves soil that other plants can easily grow in.

Pittsburgh's decaying infrastructure and abandoned buildings are ripe with metaphors about that process, and I wanted to make something that would capture those poetic thoughts about change, decay, and renewal in physical form. I see such forces at work already, so I simply gave them a physical form.

Talk to me about your creative approach to this project. How did you come up with this idea and how do you execute it?

Ever since I moved to Pittsburgh, I've thought of it as a totally creepy, decaying place. The empty steel mills, the strange, potholed streets to nowhere, the ancient brick Victorian houses, the city-owned steps that connect different neighborhoods, all of it rolls together into one big, strange, weird city. Combine that with a rather insomniacal undergraduate experience [at Carnegie Mellon University] and the idea of the city as one huge organism or ecosystem, every pore and gill brimming with delightful, disgustingly specific life-forms, from bottle caps to skyscrapers, came pretty easily.

The execution is half high-theory, half practicality. The high-theory part is that, like fungi, my materials (tempera paint and cardboard) are temporary, fleeting things that will themselves be broken down by time and weather. They are also natural pieces of the urban environment. Cardboard is an essential kind of urban trash, and cheap paint is, well, universally available in cities. I don't even know where my first tempera bottle came from, it just arrived in my life.

The practical part is that tempera and cardboard are cheap, and I don't feel bad or weird or fake trying to use them. They are a humble, almost scratch-paper-like medium.

How do you choose your buildings?

Easy. The pieces I have placed, I placed in run-down buildings that I've been watching for years. I've had for years a running list of run-down places around the city ready for art-bombing. As I create the pieces, each one seems, upon completion, to have a natural place to go to from that list. I hope the people placing my work have a similar internal notion.

How long do you keep your work in these buildings?

Until the same forces that are slowly destroying the buildings destroy the work.

What's so special about Pittsburgh? Would this project work as well in other cities?

Really any place would work, as long as there is some amount of human-created decay: abandoned train tracks, old highways, and temple ruins. Pittsburgh works well for them because it has a large concentration of abandonment, decay, and general desecration. I could see pieces in other rust belt cities (Buffalo, Detroit, Worcester, etc. . . .) with little or no change.

How many pieces have you done so far? How long do you intend to do this?

It's been a busy year with other things, so there are only twenty or so right now. I make more as I have, or carve out, time. There is no strong end date yet.

Has the community responded to your project at all? What has the response been like?

I haven't heard or read anything yet. My secret hope is that, in the middle of the night, walking home from a long, possibly terrible evening out, some half-drunk stranger catches a glimpse of one of them in the dark. I hope that, at that point, the cardboard has gotten wet and started to melt and fall apart, and that this person CANNOT tell if the horrible, black-eyed figure they see was even made by a human and not just a figment of their drunken, exhausted mind.

Update: On April 21, 2011, Connor stopped by three of the places he had put his paintings and they were all gone!

MEET THE GOAT SUCKER

BY JADE MILLER

For a fleeting moment in my childhood, I wanted to be a cryptozoologist. This was after the even more unreasonable career path of the superhero Earthra but before the practical choice of marine biologist. Cryptozoologists study cryptids, which are creatures whose presence has been suggested but is considered improbable if not impossible by the scientific community. So, you have Bigfoot, the Yeti, the Loch Ness Monster, and of course, the chupacabra.

Chupacabra literally translates to "goat sucker" in Spanish. This creature has been described in a range of ways, the most common being an animal that is reptile-like with a dog face, spines down its back, and large fangs. Unlike regular predators, the chupacabra drains its prey of blood through three holes in the shape of an upside-down triangle, which matches the way canine teeth sit in the mouth. The chupacabra also leaves behind a tell-tale sulfuric scent.

The chupacabra has mostly been spotted in Central and North America and was first seen in 1995 in Puerto Rico. This sighting accompanied the discovery of eight dead sheep, drained of their blood and with three puncture wounds in their chests. Just a few months later, again in Puerto Rico, another 150 farm animals and family pets were reportedly killed by the creature.

This creature is a celebrity in its own right with an episode of *The X-Files*, a *Scooby-Doo* movie, and, more recently, an episode of *Bones* and the video game *Red Dead Redemption: Undead Nightmare* all featuring the chupacabra.

In almost every case, the chupacabra has turned out to really be a coyote with severe parasitic mange, weakening the animal and turning its skin a bluish color. In its weakened state, the coyote preys on livestock since it's easier to bring down than wild prey.

The most recent sighting and killing of a chupacabra occurred on October 7, 2011 in Mississippi.

AN ANARCHIST FAIRY TALE

BY CHRISTINE STODDARD

E lwin Cotman's first book, *The Jack Daniels Sessions EP* (Six Gallery Press, 2010), proves that magic and grit don't have to be mutually exclusive. Writing somewhere between Toni Morrison and Hans Christian Andersen, Cotman yarns fairy tales set at D.C. punk shows and Jim Crow-era farmlands alike. And what the then twenty-six-year-old author said during our early February 2011 phone conversation indicates that his gift for negotiating the real and unreal only grows as he continues to read, live, and observe. Yet well before I spoke to Elwin on that algid evening—me in Richmond, Virginia, and him in San Francisco—I had formed an unshakable opinion of him and his talent.

Initially, I had been wary about opening Cotman's email. The email's title implied that it was a response to a Craigslist ad I had posted as a director of a non-profit arts festival. I knew from personal experience that both timid perverts and innovative artists alike lurk on CL. Who would respond when was always a toss-up. But, eh, I shrugged, there was no harm in reading an email.

Cotman had visited the art festival's website and was disappointed that he had missed the annual event. He asked if he could participate next year. So far, so good. I kept reading.

Then Cotman said he was touring across the South with his in-development book. He did not know anyone in Richmond, but, after noticing that I went to school there and checking out my work online, wanted to know if I'd read with him. Pure courtesy and nothing about nude photos. My CL fears rapidly subsiding, I said yes.

At this point, I still did not know Cotman or his work. After discussing the logistics of scheduling the reading, we did not further correspond. Our reading was still a couple of months away at that point. I took a chance on a potentially mediocre writer, but the risk paid off. On July 31, 2010, Elwin Cotman read excerpts from *The Jack Daniel Sessions EP* at Chop Suey Books in Carytown, and I was astounded. Aliens and anarchists interacting in a way that makes sense? Wow. This was a first-time-soon-to-be-published-author? Double wow.

I arrived at Chop Suey about thirty minutes before the reading. Looking like a packrat, I was holding boxes full of art prints and comics to sell after the reading. I threw them down with a sigh of relief, nervously repositioned the chairs in the room and sat down. Cotman came maybe ten minutes later.

Somehow, from the moment I saw him, I perceived his vast sensitivity. I would later see that same sensitivity in his writing, when he was able to inhabit the minds of both children and supernatural creatures. Cotman had the aura of one of those rare people who's capable of both thinking and feeling profoundly. Maybe agreeing to this reading wasn't the worst idea, after all. I could learn from this fella.

Cotman is not a tall man or big in any sense of the word's literal definition, but he is striking. He has pecan skin with cinnamon freckles and a deep auburn mini-Afro. At the time, Cotman was clean-shaven. A smile rested naturally on his face. Despite the fact that he had been traveling for a while at that point, he dressed sharply with a crisp white dress shirt, formal pants, and a feathered fedora.

Immediately, Cotman spoke kindly and evenly. After politely introducing ourselves, we discussed how to split up our reading time and soon started to address our modest audience.

I gathered then what I know for certain now that I have had a chance to read *Jack Daniels* from cover to cover. The book is riveting, engaging, a page-turner—whatever best translates into "a flurry of fascinating subjects, themes, emotions, and conflicts." Think ghosts, teen angst, racism, poverty, Adams Morgan, virginity, harpies, the Bible, World War I, and far more. *Jack Daniels* features five stories: "Safe Space," "When the Law Come," "Dead Teenagers," "How Brother Roy Lost His Dog, Twice," and "Assistant." While their characters are rich and varied, all of the stories exemplify Cotman's strong hold of concepts involving the imaginary, the nostalgic, and the otherworldly.

Michael S. Begnal, author of *Ancestor Worship*, put his praise of *Jack Daniels* as such:

"Cotman's interests are wide-ranging: Punk rock intersects with D.C.'s Dominican community, African-American folktale intersects with Greek myth, Goth teen suburban angst in 1990s Ohio sits side by side with racist atrocity in the pre-Civil Rights South . . . Yeah, there's magic in some of these stories, but the real magic is in Cotman's words themselves—stark and deadpan one moment, lushly descriptive the next."

"Safe Space" and "Dead Teenagers" take place in the 1990s, whereas the rest of the stories take place from the 1920s to '60s. The former use modern and fairly standard English sprinkled with some punk terms and numerous musical references. Punk music is clearly important to Cotman and his characters. During our February phone interview, he described music in general as "an incredibly cerebral art form" and explains that he is "intensely jealous of anyone who plays an instrument."

But words are Cotman's instruments. There is certainly nothing awkward about the way he employs them, either. "When the Law Come," "How Brother Roy Lost His Dog, Twice," and "Assistant" all make eloquent and often humorous yet touching use of poor, unlearned African-American dialect. The diction is powerful and the stories themselves are magnetic.

While I could not choose a favorite story in the book, the one that most resonates with me is "Assistant." This is most likely because it is the longest and therefore the most absorbing. It is hard to forget sixty-four enthralling pages about a young black boy whose job it is to collect the inner-children of those who have died and lead them to the afterlife at the same time that he is witnessing the horrific effects of white Southern racism on his sharecropping community.

Cotman is not an autobiographical writer, but he pays tribute to the adage of "writing what you know." The story "Dead Teenagers," for instance, evolved out of a stint in high school detention (but it was "not cool like Breakfast Club," he quipped over a the wail of a siren). A decade ago, he was sitting next to a girl who had recently broken up with his friend. That same girl was mourning the loss of a classmate who had just died in a moped accident. It was an incident that had affected everyone in his class, but this girl seemed particularly shaken. Cotman snatched up that real-life instance of drama and made it his own, ghosts and all.

"A fairy tale is a very stripped-down kind of story," Cotman said in his authoritative yet unobtrusive way. "Fairy tales are about getting caught up in the storytelling."

He went on to say that while myths are common to all societies, that does not make them trite. It makes them relevant to all of humanity. "The state of fantasy literature is very exciting right now," he gushed (but only a little), "because people are reinventing old myths." Again, Cotman spoke almost as if he did not include himself in this pool of incredibly gifted people, yet to think of him as a non-member would be a huge mistake.

On a note aside from Cotman's captivating writing, it would be unforgivable not to mention the illustrations in *Jack Daniels*. While not responsible for their creation, Cotman thought very carefully about which artist he would choose to visually interpret his stories. He eventually picked Rachel Dorrett, a native of Baltimore who, like Cotman, adores fantasy-based work.

As a whole, Cotman truly values collaboration between writers and other artists. He believes that "any kind of art you do is storytelling" and champions "the ability to meld different art forms" as "amazing." From now on, he intends to have an artist illustrate every one of his books. Cotman definitely wants to include more song and music in his readings, too.

With the sounds of San Francisco traffic blaring as he paused to think, Cotman overshadowed the noise with "It's really easy for people to lose interest if you're just reading at them." (As if to say his words were merely words).

Even as a boy, Cotman was interested in collaboration and experimenting with other art forms. He and his younger sister would launch into oral fan fiction using characters from their favorite Judy Blume books. His father gave him a typewriter to play with and read young Elwin stories as he punched at its keys. Meanwhile, his mother gave him cassettes and Cotman used them to record the stories he made up throughout the day.

Cotman also thanks his family for introducing him to so many books, movies, and TV shows as a child. Cotman's welding of magic, history, and anarcho-punk culture stem from his early loves of everything from Tolkien to Scorsese to The Cure to Nintendo and more—as long as a good story was involved.

As Cotman aged, he refined his tastes and honed his storytelling. At age twelve, he won a poetry contest judged by August Wilson. Throughout high school, he took journalism classes. Then in 2003, he enrolled at the University of Pittsburgh and eventually graduated with a degree in fiction writing.

From there he had many adventures in Washington, D.C., Pittsburgh, and San Francisco, hopping between the three areas whenever he saw fit. While he recently completed his third semester at Mills College, Cotman began his M.F.A. at the University of Maryland. He was also, at one point, the writer-in-residence at The Cyberpunk Apocalypse Writer's Project in Pittsburgh. Cotman has been, according to the biography printed at the end of *Jack Daniels*, "a Wal-Mart employee, bookseller, middle school teacher, youth counselor and ESL instructor." Each job allowed him to do what he treasures most: write.

In 2009, Cotman launched an ambitious series of readings in Pittsburgh. The one that made a professional difference happened in an art gallery called Modern Formations. It was there that Che Elias, publisher and editor of Six Gallery Press, heard him read. Then and there, Elias asked him if he had a book in the works. The answer was yes and—boom!—that project was *Jack Daniels*.

Remarkably, the oldest story in *Jack Daniels* dates back to 2003, which Cotman began as a college freshman, whereas the newest one was born in 2008, not too long before Six Gallery Press took notice of his unique voice and subject matter.

Six Gallery has been a boutique independent publishing company since 2000. They only publish fiction and poetry, and typically take interest in talented Pittsburghers. Thus, their philosophy, like Cotman's, is very community-minded.

"I value the community part of writing . . . workshopping is incredibly integral to the process," Cotman said. That is precisely why he appreciates the M.F.A. program at Mills: he is surrounded by other writers. He's also living in a hippie house in San Francisco, which only adds to the creative forces he constantly craves in his life.

Apart from promoting his book, Cotman's latest endeavor is a radio show called Fort Liberty. He describes it as "a historical drama/epic/soap opera" about a forty-something anarchist living in Pittsburgh. He's banking on San Francisco's creative spirit to make it a reality. Once again, the community may just come to his rescue and spot his knack for "spinning a good yarn" which is his main goal in all he does.

The last time I saw Cotman (only the second time in my life) was at my own reading. I was recovering from a nasty bout of food poisoning when the day I'd been anticipating for months finally arrived. Per his suggestion, I had applied to the residency program at The Cyberpunk Apocalypse Writer's Project. From mid-December to mid-January, I wrote and illustrated a book project. January 14 marked the culmination of my efforts, and I felt like swallowing my tongue.

Cotman, on the other hand, looked comfortable, casual. Punk but not "fashion punk." No mohawk, no challenging-the-status-quo type piercings. He looked more like a thrift shop punk in his burgundy hoodie, worn jeans, dark shoes, and woven ski cap. He plopped down onto a tweed armchair with plush poking out from its jarring pores and holes like pus.

Sleepy-eyed and not especially fast to speak, Cotman was still adjusting to the time difference between San Francisco and bone-biting Pittsburgh, where his relatives lived.

As people trickled into the communal room, Cotman looked far too reserved for a man whose book release was only about a week away. *Jack*

Daniels' launch party was scheduled for January 22 in Oakland, CA. But when I spoke to Cotman a week or so after the party, he was not quite so tame. He was ecstatic:

"The book doesn't suck. I love all of the stories for entirely different reasons. I am intensely excited about how the book came out. Anyone who enjoys storytelling will enjoy this book."

And don't we all enjoy a good story?

OLD-TIMEY S-E-X

BY JOSEPHINE STONE

The Victorian era, defined as the period between 1837 and 1901 during the reign of Queen Victoria, was a time of great sexual awakening in women. During this period, women's roles changed drastically from censored and submissive to educated owners of their bodies. The changes to the Victorian female—beautiful, childbearing property that need remain sexually uneducated for the sake of fidelity and virginity—occurred over the century with several marriage acts and contraception. From these amendments, a sexual being was born, debunking the archetype of the Victorian lady that exists today.

Despite the modern-day sexuality tied to the image and dress of the Victorian woman, such as corsets and crinolines, the debilitating garb was an attempt to ensure a submissive, housebound female figure of the household. In the middle to upper classes, also called the "leisure class," women were valued for their beauty. As written by Fraser Harrison in *The Dark Angel*, "The ideal emphasizes their estrangement from all aspects of vulgarly productive labour . . . and concentrates . . . especially [on] the slenderness of the waist whose perfect proportions imply extreme debility." The fashion of the time included the baroque bonnet, high-heels, large skirts, and corsets, all of which proved the impracticality of doing any tasks. The important image of beauty as defined by soft hands, porcelain complexion, and dainty feet kept women in the household outside of the sun's rays and in the visually appealing clothing that served no purpose outside of emphasizing an image of sexiness to men (Harrison 34-7).

The Victorian woman was not only debilitated by her dress but also in her sexual education. Regardless of the emphasis of being attractive for men, once women were courted to be married, they were introduced to sexual intimacy for the first time. Sexual language in Victorian Britain was almost nonexistent for the idea that without vulgar or sexual language in society, the existence of vulgar, sexual behavior and desires would not be. Women of this period were also excluded from discussions in institutions and intellectual discourse that kept them from any understanding of sexual behavior even in scientific means (Clark 115-9). In addition to their beauty, women were to receive little education, and were to be "lethargic young women in whom the virtues of decorous idleness and pretty ignorance had been so assiduously inculcated" (Harrison 30).

The preservation of the "pure" minds of women lead to problems that would affect their relationships with their husbands and inhibit women's understanding of their own changing bodies. If the topic of female sexuality was discussed at all, it was done in a manner that made reproduction a topic of disgust, causing women to behave as though humans' erotic qualities did not exist. It was this lack of erotic reality in their minds that ensured virginity and fidelity, for a woman without acceptance of her own sexuality couldn't possibly put it at risk (Harrison 55). Besides being completely ignorant about reproduction and the effects of puberty on their bodies, many were disgusted, disappointed, or shocked upon entering the bridal bed.

Most knowledge of women's reactions to sexual behavior during the Victorian era is taken from letters in which women wrote to each other of their love, anger, and common emotions that, at the time, weren't permitted to be openly expressed. A young Emily Austin wrote a letter describing the disappointment she felt upon her wedding night, after her marriage to John Austin. She described their honeymoon as "a nightmare of physical pain and mental disappointment" because John had intercourse quickly and without sensitivity (Clark 123). Emily voiced her frustration over not being able to change their sex life because she believed she was unable to make sexual demands.

Other exceptions to the rule existed with women who felt an unexplained lack in their relationship with their new husbands, only to learn later about sexual intimacy and realize they had experienced none. A young Effie Gray annulled her marriage of six years to John Ruskin in 1848 after being refused sexual consummation. Effie wrote her parents of her anger toward John for not having sex with her, an act that showed a great deal of confidence in her own sexuality. She was not sure at first what was missing in their relationship, writing to her parents, "I had never been told the duties of married persons to each other" (Clark 122). A similar situation and annulment occurred between a Marie Stopes and a Dr. Reginald Ruggles Gates in 1911. Six months after their marriage, Marie began to "feel instinctively that something was lacking" and visited the British Museum to learn about sex. Marie ended up suing for an annulment on the grounds that she was virgo intacta and later published *Married Love* in 1918. The option to annul a marriage on such terms, however, was a new development, and at the beginning of the Victorian era, a woman could be arrested for denying her husband his conjugal rights, losing her complete legal existence once married (Harrison 7, 50-1).

Other financially and socially powerful women provided another archetype of Victorian female sexuality after matrimony. Queen Victoria, aside from being royalty, was vastly different from most women during the beginning of the sexual revolution of her rule for the fact that she never had to submit to the will and standards of her husband, Albert. Queen Victoria ruled England and had no ruler or master in social and sexual servitude as most women did after marriage. Queen Victoria's power allowed her to make a decision about how she would act during their sexual encounters, and Harrison writes that "On the few occasions when she felt she could afford to behave toward Albert in a purely wifely capacity, she displayed a surprising submissiveness," continuing on to say that Victoria was unrelenting in her "determination to keep the word 'obey' in their marriage service" (Harrison 25). Given that she was a woman of power, we can assume that keeping her public role and her marital role separate was of utmost importance. Therefore, she chose to follow the common standard of submissiveness when appropriate.

Where relationships with men and husbands failed, women found solace in each other, sometimes sprouting sexual relationships in a manner that seemed common at the time. Many women of the Victorian age lived together, shared property, described one another as spouses, and went as far as to make vows of fidelity to one another. Once women were vowed to one another, they were also considered spouses by their social network, and their relationship mimicked the legal marriages between men and women. A perfect example of a marriage between women in Victorian England can be found in the relationships had by a Charlotte Cushman, an acclaimed actress of the nineteenth-century. Most documented sexual encounters in Charlotte's diary are between her and other women; she wrote in 1844, "Slept with Rose," a name mentioned several times before in her diary. A few days later an entry reads, "Married." The diary never describes the outcome of her "marriage" with Rose, and later Charlotte had two long-term relationships, among many other, short term ones, with a Matilda Hays and an Emma Stebbins. Sharon Marcus, author of *Between Women*, writes that Charlotte's sexual behavior as a whole was "matrilineal, incestuous, adulterous, polygamous and homosexual"—all traits that defied the conservative notions of what love, marriage, and family could be. "Patriarchal monogamy does not contain the promiscuity that results when women reign unfettered," Marcus continues (Marcus 145-7). Marcus' harsh description of the sexual freedom and promiscuity of Charlotte is given alongside written letters that prove her incestuous relationship with a young woman named Emma Crow, whom Charlotte convinced to marry her nephew so that she and Emma would be able to spend time together sexually and as a family.

Social marriages between women seemed a common occurrence, and the widespread knowledge and acceptance of Charlotte and her endeavors can be credited to her high social standing. As a popular actress, Charlotte had financial independence and did not need to marry a man to gain wealth or social standing. In this vein, marriage between women was mostly common between ladies of the middle and upper classes. In a time before legislation granted women legal and property rights, these were women who did not have as dire a need to elevate their standing by marrying a man, thereby becoming property and completely dependent post-matrimony.

Near the end of the Victorian era, advances in women's rights were made through the passing of several acts. With a prevalence of prostitution, pleasure-seeking men, and a lack of scientific knowledge on the topic, venereal disease posed a threat to many women. In addition, the threat of pregnancy also kept women from having sex for the sake of pleasure, in contrast to the motives of most men at the time. In Hera Cook's book, *The Long Sexual Revolution*, Cook writes, "Contraception and pregnancy take place within the female body," whereas for men, "coitus was assumed to be the aim of sexual desire." This double standard, as well as women's legal inability to deny their husbands their conjugal rights, prevented most Victorian women from seeking pleasure in sexual intimacy. This all changed, however, in the late 1800s with the invention and widespread use of contraceptives, as well as the Divorce Act of 1857, the Married Women's Property Bill of 1857, and the Matrimonial Causes Acts of 1870, 1882, and 1893, which established equal social standards for both parties and granted women rights to property, legal proceedings, and contracts.

As the rights of the Victorian woman slowly came to pass, the sexual revolution and emphasis on the importance of the female orgasm rapidly gained traction. The newfound freedom of sexual education and the idea of feminine sex for pleasure prevailed through government rescinding of obscenity restrictions and laws. Literature and familial discourse about sex still being limited, museums remained one of the only places where detailed models of genitalia could be found. The London Museum was closed in 1873 due to anti-obscenity laws that disagreed with the display. Also, during the period when women were gaining rights, a flurry of pamphlets entitled "Aristotle's Masterpiece" that focused on fertility were widely circulated, going so far as to describe sexual pleasure and the female orgasm to be detrimental to conception, sparking the Obscene Publications Act of 1857 (Clark 115-6).

With the use of contraceptives, the birth rate fell from 1871 to 1900, and, according to Harrison, "For the first time in the history of monogamy, wives had obtained the means of liberating themselves from the tyranny of reproduction, and they could at last regard their husbands' sexual attentions as a medium of pleasure, and to respect, not fear, their sexuality" (Harrison 67). It took time for men to adjust to women's newfound sexual pleasure, self respect, and social independence. What had once been a man's property, to be used for his own pleasure, now became a demanding, pleasure-driven being that could legally take action against him. During the late 1800s when the sexual hierarchy was shifting, the economy was unstable, adding to the anxiety of the men of Victorian England. Many men did not know how to react to the sudden aggressive nature in which women sought equal emotional and sexual relations (Harrison 118).

An example of men's baffled reactions to aggressive female sexuality can be found in the writings of a William Hazlitt, who describes a young woman by the name of Sarah Walker, the daughter of a lodging housekeeper. Upon a stay at the lodge, William wrote that Sarah would "be sitting in my lap, twining herself around me . . . rubbing against [me]" for an hour. When he brought up the idea of marriage to her, she was disinterested and replied, "Why could we not go on as we were and nevermind about the word forever?" William, perhaps like many men of the period, associated her sexual desire with prostitution, and tried to offer her money when she denied him her hand in marriage. Sarah also refused to be bought. These writings that describe a woman who wanted sex for what it was, and not for money or marriage, provide a revisionist view of female sexuality during the Victorian era, where most constructs describe Victorian women as exceptionally prudish or anxious (Clark 125-7). It was this total shift in the stereotype of women's sexuality that caused many men to alter their own understanding of sexuality, and "an equation between sexual pleasure and emotional fulfillment crystallized in their mind" (Harrison 133). In this manner, the sexual awakening of women also allowed for a greater understanding of sexual relationships for men as well.

Modern perceptions of Victorian female sexuality are mostly derived from the early years—we imagine a proper lady, lacking vulgar thought and action, beautified by the layers of lace and corset that ties her waist. It was during this period, however, women shifted from playing the limited role of daughter or wife in the primitive family portrait to being active seekers of property and pleasure. Due to censorship of sexual discourse and the notion that marital sexual relations should be limited to childbearing, the Victorian lady remained, in the earlier years, completely in the dark when it came to sex. The bridal bed was a disheartening learning experience for many new wives, and social marriages between women abounded. With the many acts passed in the mid-eighteenth century, women finally found and respected their own sexualities, thereby changing the role of the Victorian woman to account for her emotional and educational needs, and providing a lesson for the men of the period as well.

WEREWOLF WOE

BY MICHELLE LABBE

Werewolves always get the short end of the stick. Or at least it seems that way sometimes. Time and time again, werewolves are pitted against vampires in the battle for our cultural affection, and time and again they're shunted aside, playing a perpetual second fiddle to the children of the night. Somehow, it's the vampire who always gets the girl, not the werewolf. (Even when the vampire's a sparkly wuss and the werewolf rides a sweet motorcycle.) *Buffy the Vampire Slayer*'s token werewolf, Oz, is at least sympathetic, and he even snags resident overachiever Willow for his girlfriend, but he disappears after Season 4 while the vampire Angel gets a whole spin-off to himself in which to vent his angst. Don't even get me started on the fate of Remus Lupin. Werewolves deserve more. They deserve better.

I've been researching werewolf literature out of the conviction that there must be more out there. That there must be stories in which the werewolf wins, where the werewolf is more human than beast. Werewolf legends are essentially about human nature, about the battle between society's mores and our more primal impulses, about losing control and giving in to anger or fear or sexual desire, about how we all go a little mad sometimes. Oddly enough, everything we think we know about werewolves—the silver bullets, the transformation by moonlight, that whole business with the pentagrams—comes from the cinematic tradition of the 1930s, Universal creature flicks. The earliest appearances of werewolves in literature reach far back in time—the earliest mention is in Petronius' *Satyricon*—and draw on a different set of traditions and beliefs, ones that the tropes of Universal Films, like *The Wolf Man*, replaced in our cultural consciousness.

One of the earliest werewolf tales, "Bisclavret," appears in one of the twelfth-century lais in *The Lais of Marie de France*. Marie explains in an aside that a werewolf is a "ferocious beast," possessed by madness, who "devours men, causes great damage, and dwells in vast forests." "Bisclavret" itself is a poem about a knight, Bisclavret, beloved by all but hiding the secret of his lycanthropy. In this tale, werewolves transform weekly rather than according to the lunar cycle, living as wolves for three days of the week and as humans for the rest. Here, the werewolf form is also significantly more vulnerable than in modern lore: Bisclavret's wife betrays him by stealing his human clothes while he is in the shape of a wolf; without his clothes, he cannot change back. Clothing, the outward trappings of civilization, become the key to humanity. Without his clothing, Bisclavret must wander naked in the woods, trapped in inhumanity, unable to regain his senses.

Later renditions of werewolves adhere to similar principles: transformation is performed consciously, often through the donning of wolf-skins or simply through belts made of wolf-skin. Where transformation was linked to a particular time, it was linked to the passing of the seasons rather than the phases of the moon until 1943's *Frankenstein Meets the Wolf Man*. And the concept of lycanthropy not as hereditary but as a disease—an infection spread by the bite of another werewolf—seems to have first appeared in *The Werewolf of London* in which the protagonist was the victim of a Gypsy werewolf's bite. In either mythos, the transformation tends to be about unleashing the "beast within," the darker side of human nature. There is a pulp fiction tradition of werewolves who prey on female victims. These werewolves are, if a little hirsute, also seductive and charismatic, tempting legions of Little Red Riding Hoods to stray from their paths. In older legends, werewolves are demonic servants of the Devil, as in the tales of female were-witches who raid the countryside, until one of their husbands discovers her in animal form and shoots her paw, only to discover the next day that his own wife bears a wounded hand.

But is that all there is to werewolves? Hardly. Modern revisionist fantasy literature, while it takes more effort to uncover, often makes an eloquent case for sympathy for the werewolf in stories like Angela Carter's film *In the Company of Wolves*, where Red Riding Hood goes willingly to sleep with the wolf in his bed, or her short story "Wolf Alice,", where the half-human girl shows more humanity than any of the townsfolk. There's also Annette Curtis Klause's novel *Blood and Chocolate*, about a teenaged female werewolf who revels in her dual nature. *Buffy the Vampire Slayer* and *Harry Potter* are less forthcoming; both portray the werewolf as one who loses all humanity during the wolf phase of transformation, however good-natured in human form. The werewolves of Terry Pratchett's *Discworld* series are a mixed bag: some are good and even use their wolfish traits for good—Angua of the City Watch uses her enhanced sense of smell to solve crime—but she is an outlier; all her family are werewolves of the monstrous, beastly variety.

But why, even in with increasingly sympathetic portrayals, do werewolves always seem to get short shrift, especially when vampires hit the scene? Maybe it's the fur, the slobber; they cannot be as charming as the suave, sophisticated vampire with slicked-back hair and a silken cravat, plying his intended victim with wine before turning his attentions to her smooth neck. And yet werewolves used to be more popular: the *Wolf Man* series put out by Universal Pictures comprised the most popular of the monster movies, eclipsing both the *Frankenstein* and *Dracula* franchises. Perhaps werewolves suffer from the lack of a basic generative text, one that is present for Frankenstein's creature and for Dracula. Modern werewolf stories draw mainly from a set of essentially inauthentic film scripts from seventy or eighty years ago, though admittedly, *Frankenstein* and *Dracula* are not so much older themselves. Still, either story draws on rich backgrounds of lore and legend (not for nothing does *Frankenstein* bear the subtitle "A Modern Prometheus") rather than inventing new tropes wholesale, as the *Wolf Man* films do.

Sam Merlotte pines for Sookie on *True Blood*, but his were-collie doesn't hold a candle to brooding vampire Bill. Oz is eventually replaced in Willow's affections, though the replacement, Tara, is winsome enough to withstand any strong objections. But there is hope: in *Harry Potter*, Tonks loves Lupin as man and wolf, and *Blood and Chocolate*'s Vivian finds love too, if not in the place she expected. Maggie Stiefvater's exciting new werewolf trilogy, one that reverts to the medieval tradition as a source for its werewolf mythos, also holds promise for werewolves who won't finish last. Where the literature is still lacking, let us take that as a challenge: as a call to write it ourselves, expand it to fulfill our own needs. Every werewolf should have his day in the sun.

KIBBUTZ!

BY JULIE DINISIO

Peace, love, and communal living: hippie communes didn't die out with the 1960s. In fact, the Fellowship for Intentional Communities lists hundreds of communities across the United States, many of which are currently in the process of forming. The term "hippie" has ceased to truly define the majority of these places, though, and most fall under the category of "intentional community."

Just like drug use, communal living wasn't a novelty in the 1960s—it just became a stereotype for the decade. To trace the roots of these communities, one could go back for centuries. European in origin, commune leaders found new possibilities for their radical ideas in the New World. Author Joseph Manzella gave these reasons as to why America has been fertile soil for communes: "the availability of natural resources, the political structures of Europe, the nature of colonial settlement, and the freedom to slip between the cracks of societies in the making."

Robert Owen, a native of Wales, succeeded in falling "between the cracks" of American society in 1825 when he started New Harmony. An enthusiastic socialist, Owen began this colony of 180 buildings set on 30,000 acres of Indiana land. After putting his son in charge of New Harmony, Owen toured the United States seeking financial backers for his eight-hundred-member and growing community. Structural problems caused New Harmony to close in 1828, but Owen's socially progressive ideas have influenced many of today's labor laws and educational programs.

Twenty years after New Harmony's dissolution, John Humphrey Noyes began Oneida, a Perfectionist community that, as the name would indicate, focused on self-perfection. Noyes introduced the idea of open heterosexual relationships, a feature that is still affiliated with some communes today. Because outside society was unwilling to accept these "complex marriages," Oneida suffered the same fate as New Harmony.

Through the decades, America saw a variety of other communities form and dissolve. Massachusetts's Brook Farm attracted famous transcendentalists like Nathaniel Hawthorne; the French Icarians settled in Texas, Illinois, and California; the Amish even constitute an example of communal life—one of the most successful ones, actually. Attempts at utopia exploded in the 1960s, though, as communes formed under the labels of gay liberation, opposition to the war in Vietnam, and occultism. Robert P. Sutton, an expert on secular communities, declared this form of communalism "drug tolerant protests of the counterculture." He went on to say, "Young men and women both single and married, 'dropped out' to experience a communal psychology of self-actualization."

In America today, there's an unprecedented variety of intentional communes which stretch from Hawaii to the backyard of Richmond, Virginia. Twin Oaks Intentional Community is located in Louisa County, Virginia, and claims ninety-five residents. Established in 1967, it's one of the oldest communes in existence, and on Saturdays from March through October, anyone can take a three-hour tour of the sprawling 450 acres.

Wizard, a nine-year resident of the commune and the guide of these informative tours, declared Twin Oaks the "mother ship of all communes." He went on to speak for himself and his fellow residents when he said, "We choose to live here because it's so different from the mainstream world."

Twin Oaks Intentional Community is rustic and quiet, lending a peaceful atmosphere to the wood buildings, dirt paths, and gardens. Residents are expected to work at least forty-two hours a week in any of the commune's many businesses. Twin Oaks generates most of its revenue through making hammocks and tofu. Currently in the process of expanding the tofu business to meet a growing demand, the managers are hoping to soon produce 20,000 pounds of it a day. The product can be found in Whole Foods Markets in Charlottesville and Richmond.

Though Twin Oaks makes an estimated million dollars a year, money is not its focus. Those earnings go back into the income-sharing community and into a savings account for the aging members. The community members are currently building a hospice for the elderly and sick people. As Wizard said, "We want to take care of everybody when they're functional but also when they're non-functional."

Twin Oaks interacts very little with the local government and is governed by a planner-manager system. There are managers of each area of the commune who make decisions that can be contested by anyone. A planner is a member that steps up to act as a mediator until an issue is resolved.

Twin Oaks neither discourages nor forbids drug use. According to Wizard, use is not nearly as rampant as the stereotype would suggest due to the lack of money and the personal beliefs of the residents. Though he did add that the community is a "microcosm of the world. Everything that happens in the real world happens here."

All of the buildings and dormitories on the property are named after former famous communities: Harmony, Oneida, Llano, and Aurora, to name a few. A diverse array of people shares these aptly named buildings. Men, women, children, Christians, atheists, and spiritualists all inhabit Twin Oaks. The community supports open relationships and a feminist ideal. Perhaps most notably, though, it's a self-sustaining ecovillage because of its policies on conservation, food production, and energy resources.

East Wind Community, a sister commune to Twin Oaks, was established in 1974 and is located in the Missouri Ozarks. This more rural version of Twin Oaks is non-secular and currently has forty-five members, who call mainstream society "Babylon." Charlie Flatt, a five-year resident, heard about East Wind through National Geographic, visited, and stayed.

Flatt said, "I enjoy never having to commute to work; the Ozark Mountains are beautiful, the food is great, and there are learning opportunities here not generally available to all of mainstream society." To this, he added, "We want to demonstrate that there is an alternative to the consumer society. In a community [like ours], you must develop relationships with the people you are both living and working with, which is largely absent in Babylon."

Sandhill Farm is a community that shares a few similarities with East Wind, in that it is also located in Missouri and was also established in 1974. However, Sandhill is diminutive in comparison, comprising only eight members. It's an egalitarian community (as are Twin Oaks and East Wind) that emphasizes the importance of the environment.

Laird Schaub has been a member of Sandhill since it opened almost forty years ago. He joined "to recapture the stimulation and support of dormitory living in college." He went on to say, "I've stayed because I am not aware of any lifestyle that provides these things better. I enjoy how work is shared and how each member has a high degree of work they like doing."

Sandhill is an organically certified farm set on about 120 acres. The residents farm the land, participate in agricultural studies, and keep bees. Schaub attested Sandhill's principles by saying, "Our values are to provide a high quality of life for each member, steward the land responsibly, and minimize our impact on the environment."

Twin Oaks, East Wind, and Sandhill are all examples of religiously open, multi-purpose communes, but many are far narrower in focus. Tomorrow's Bread Today, for example, is a Christian cooperative, in which money is collected and pooled from members to evenly distribute healthcare. Justseeds Artists' Cooperative is based in Pennsylvania but boasts members from all over North America who create politically and socially radical artwork.

Many communities don't last beyond one generation and end in failure—overly idealistic worlds unable to sustain themselves. There's a logical reason for this, as many children of commune dwellers choose to leave the alternative lifestyle. The fact that so many 1960s communities were abandoned could be because "the baby boomers were the last American generation to be raised with the idea of limitless possibilities," as Joseph Manzella ascertains. The idealism for alternative lifestyles simply was not passed on to the next generation.

Another reason for failure could be the lack of diversity found in communities. While most promote racial tolerance, the majority of residents are white, middle class, and well-educated. Manzella attributes this to a difference in priorities between members and minorities. On the other hand, Wizard from Twin Oaks believes it to be a difference in family life, saying, "White people are looking for something that many other cultures have with their families: a community."

Another expert on the intricacies of communal living, Ernest S. Wooster attributes the failure of some communes to a lack of structure and central thought through a charismatic leader or a driving purpose: "A successful non-religious colony must be one which substitutes a religious zeal towards its principles and an intelligent purpose of eliminating personal selfishness." Careless admittance to a commune—"half-baked idealists, impractical visionaries, persons seeking an easy life, and those who are unwilling to accept the hard conditions"—can also be a cause for failure, according to Wooster.

The pattern of generational problems and a lack of racial diversity will probably continue to haunt communes. However, those with a central focus (as in religion or the environment) have and will probably continue to find the most success. As the American economy changes and the market for local goods and produce continues to grow, certain types of communal living should flourish and provide a haven for those seeking a radically alternative lifestyle.

DELVING INTO
ABORIGINAL DREAMINGS
BY MARI PACK

O n the first day of my Contemporary Aboriginal Art Class at Melbourne University in Melbourne, Australia, our professor, a non-Aboriginal former-photographer-turned-art-historian, calmly but earnestly explained to us in her soft, East Coast twang that we really needed only one tool with which to encounter Aboriginal Art and Culture: respect.

Respect? I thought to myself. I'm so good at respect! I'm going to respect the crap out of this art.

As an American with little to no previous indigenous knowledge outside the sporadic *Crocodile Dundee* viewings on Comedy Central, I was determined to not just perform well but to conquer Aboriginal Art, to learn all that I possibly could. I wanted to fly back to America with the confidence that I had learned something truly unique at the edge of the world and that I had mastered it.

Eager to share my enthusiasm, I met with my professor after the lecture. I proudly proclaimed that I was just on my way to the library right now, as a matter of fact, to find some books about Aboriginal mythology. I explained to her that I would make it my mission to learn everything I could about Aboriginal culture. I would go above and beyond to comprehend the various stories and symbols that illuminated themselves through Aboriginal art.

"Dreamings," she said.

"What?"

"Not mythology—they're called Dreamings." She smiled, but it was clear that she was bracing herself. "I'm sorry to tell you, but unless you're a ritually inaugurated senior man, it's going to be very difficult for you to learn."

"Oh," I said, alarmed. She clearly did not understand the depth of my dedication. "But I really, really want to."

She smiled again. "Well, good luck with that."

The books in the Melbourne University Library that reference Aboriginal Dreamings watershed into two discernible categories: truly gaudy children's books with semi-whimsical, wholly-insulting illustrations of naked black men, women, and children encountering various totemic beings; and published anthropological dissertations with brief outlines on the general Dreamings for specific language groups. Nowhere did there exist a definitive Encyclopaedia of all, or even most, of the major Dreamings for Australian Aborigines.

I have found there to be, by and large, two main reasons for this, the first being most obvious but, sadly, one that is often overlooked. All told, there are a lot of Dreamings. Heaps of Dreamings! It has been noted that certain parts of Australia harbor more cultural diversity than all of Europe combined. Specific languages have certain Dreamings associated with them as do most places and kin groups. There are layers upon layers of varied, complex Dreaming stories passed down to through the community based on gender, kinship, and age—multiply that by the hundreds (seven hundred by last count) of language groups and you get a rough estimate of just how vast the Dreaming field really is.

The second reason for the lack of holistic documentation is the necessarily secretive nature of Aboriginal culture, which is so sacred among the Indigenous peoples of Australia that it is difficult to find a Western Equivalent. Stories are important. Not everyone is ready to hear them all. Children's stories are, as in Western cultures, the most basic. Children are taught the fundamental tales of the major characters. Most written recordings of Aboriginal Dreamings by white Australians are children's Dreamings. Then come Women's Dreamings, or "Women's Business," which often but not always, relate to "bush tucker"—plants and vegetables. Men's Dreamings, or "Men's Business," are the most secret and sacred, though both men and women of senior status maintain stories of crucial importance to the community.

The Dreamings themselves exist in continuum. The era known as the Dreamtime is the rough equivalent of Biblical genesis, when the totemic beings—the Lightning Men, the Wagilag Sisters, and the famous Rainbow Serpents—made their way across the land, shaping it and giving it life and substance.

In its most basic form, the Rainbow Serpent Dreaming explains the formation of the Australian landscape. It details how the Rainbow Serpent slithered out of her burrow to awaken the sleeping earth. As she crawled across the land, she left indentations with her body until she grew tired and slept. There are regional variations of this Dreamtime based on environmental differences. In one, the Rainbow Serpent tickles the stomachs of frogs, which are filled with water, causing them to regurgitate the water into streams across the land.

At her core, the Rainbow Serpent is a protector spirit who watches over people, and she is also a judge who punishes those who do not uphold her laws. She gives mankind its totemic beings, which tie them to the land. She gives Australia to the Australians.

It is easy to fall in love with such stories, to demand more. But the Dreamings belong to their people. This is something with which Western culture has had trouble coming to grips. For Americans, "to respect" often means "to learn about." The prominence of Black, Hispanic, and Jewish History Months exemplifies the obsession with tolerance through understanding—and more often through a deluge of information.

It is not part of the Aboriginal mind-set to horde. Everything is shared. Albert Namatjira, Australia's first nationally famous Aboriginal watercolor painter, single-handedly provided for six hundred people at the peak of his success.

In similar fashion, Aborigines have indeed begun to share their knowledge and their stories with white Australia, but slowly, as a parent would to a child, spoon-feeding. We are not ready for the great, complex Dreamings of ritually inaugurated men and women, nor are we entitled to them. To respect it is to learn, but it is not up to us what we are invited to learn.

"WONDERMARK" GETS REAL

BY CHRISTINE STODDARD

He finds charming, romantic illustrations from bygone days, manipulates them in Photoshop, and produces comics teeming with caustic characters. His name is David Malki ! (space and exclamation mark required) and his brainchild is the ever-amusing comic, *Wondermark*. Obsessed with the Victorian era but also a fan of less-than-prudish sarcasm, Malki ! is a pioneer in that field where found art and sequential art intersect. He is also a champion of web comics and alternative weekly newspapers and a man who believes in both magic and modernity. Like his comic, he is many things. But why bother with any more metaphors and adjectives? Here's what Malki ! had to say in response to Quail Bell's plethora of eagerly spat questions on fairy tales, the Victorian era, and, yes, his art:

What about the Victorian age appeals to you?

My work draws heavily on the arts and aesthetic of the era, and I'm particularly fond of the craftsmanship that went into the engravings and illustrations that fill Victorian publications. This was a time before photography was cheap or easy to reproduce for print, so anytime an illustration was called for, an artisan had to create it, either as an ink drawing, woodcut, or engraving. There was a bit of a golden age between 1875 and 1890 when this art form reached a technical zenith . . . and then photographic technology improved in the 1890s and the more cumbersome technique (the illustrations) was rendered obsolete almost instantly as publishers raced to fill their pages with photos. And it wasn't only in the printing industry—everywhere, horses were being replaced by automobiles; craftsmen by factories; farms by cities; provincialism by the rise of mass media.

It's a period that's removed from our present world but still recognizably modern, and it's a well-documented window into human nature. We can see how the people of the time dealt with and adapted to all these amazing transitions and how decisions that they made paved the way for the society we have today.

So there's that, and also I think the drawings look cool.

Would you ever want to live in the Victorian era, if only for a day?

I think it'd be fun to step into the life of someone from the Victorian era (or any far-off era, really—not with our present understanding of convenience and technology, but rather immersed in that world and understanding it on a fundamental level . . . then I'd like to come back out and compare notes after the fact. Being a tourist is one thing, but if some dark alchemy has the power to thrust me back into a world long passed, it couldn't be too hard to throw in an extra newt and see the world as a local while we're at it.

Which Victorian artists and writers do you particularly like? How does their work affect your work, if at all?

Many of the volumes in my collection are filled with the work of artisans who toiled more or less in obscurity. Some went on to greater fame in book illustration (such as John Tenniel, who drew for *Punch* before going on to illustrate Lewis Carroll's books), and others were simply masters of the spot drawing. My favorite is probably Charles Keene, another *Punch* artist, and many of my comics feature his characters. When using images that have a very distinct visual style, I try to keep each comic internally consistent to a certain degree, so many times I'll find a piece by a certain artist, then page through the same book to find other work by the same artist to combine it with. Family reunions for the first time!

But I only even know the names of a very small number of the artists from the era—much of the work in American publications is uncredited, and in a certain way that's okay. The less context the image has, the easier it is for me to change it around and do something new with it. I love working with images from German books because when paging through, I don't get distracted reading the articles like I do with British or American books! (Though now that I have a German office mate, I do trot over to ask him for the occasional translation.)

Do you ever explore fairy tales in your work? How do you think fairy tales influenced the Victorian era and what kind of impact do they have upon your work?

Fairy tales are important to a world (like the Victorians' or ours) that places a huge emphasis on science and reason and technical advancement and solving mysteries. Those things are all wonderful, but as old gods get crowded out by better and better telescopes, the stories that explain how the Northern Lights are Valkyries dancing on the graves of the Irish get harder to hear and less likely to be repeated. With all the charging and clanging progress-machines pressing bottle caps by coal power, it's easy to feel contented, like we've got the world pretty well under control—and that's where fairy tales can keep us humble. A culture that respects the mysterious and the unknowable is a culture that can never act with impunity as the greatest power around.

I'm trying to think of some way that I can retroactively recontextualize the entirety of *Wondermark* as one enormously elaborate interweaving fairy tale. I could probably do it if it wasn't for that forty-strip run in which I methodically and exhaustively disclaimed the existence of pixies in the *Wondermark* universe. I guess we all have to learn to live with our mistakes.

What role do magic and the supernatural play in your puns and themes?

A lot of my most striking work involves monsters or chimeras or other weird, "this cannot be" elements. I think I'm drawn to that in particular because the source material, very realistically rendered illustrations, gains a certain power when it's used to portray unrealistic things. It's almost like giving these creatures a stamp of authenticity, as if there really were hippo-headed giants and bird-riding warriors and Piranhasmoose that sat for portraits 120 years ago. And I like playing in a sandbox in which anything is possible. Readers never know what to expect when they come to read Wondermark and having the work occupy a world where absolutely anything can happen keeps things interesting for the readers and me both.

Now imagine that I am a bear, saying all that. See? It STILL WORKS.

How do you think comics and sequential art have evolved since the Victorian era?

Comic strips (the precursor to comic books as we know them) didn't come into being until the early twentieth century, but you can see antecedents of comics in the Victorian era. *Punch* was doing humorous single-panel illustrations with captions in the mid-nineteenth century, and once the market for documentary illustration flattened out (with the advent of photography), all those highly-trained artists had to do something with their time. Many who worked drawing houses for Harper's in the 1890s went on to draw comics in the 1910s, and in the Hearst days of newspaper wars and ubiquitous mass media, comics and magazine gag cartoons were tremendously popular and, for some artists, tremendously lucrative. But that all came later! You can see precursors to the multi-panel strip here and there in the 1800s: a gag cartoon might be broken into six panels on a page, each with a caption, explaining how some poor fellow's vacation got worse and worse.

In *Wondermark*, by taking the format and vernacular of a contemporary comic strip and populating it with characters and imagery from the Victorian era, it becomes something new—comics in the Victorian era (such as they were) didn't look much like they do today. That's kind of exciting to me! Sort of like introducing an old farmer to a modern grocery store or putting a Model T engine in a DeLorean. Wait—that wouldn't work at all. What I do is like putting a Zeppelin engine in a DeLorean. Perfect.

What advice do you have for people who want to buy Victorian illustrations like the ones you use in your work?

They are not as difficult to find as you might think! Most of the images I use for *Wondermark* are magazine and newspaper illustrations, and a lot of that material is available as bound library editions. I do a lot of research in my local library's microfilm periodicals archive, and it's also fun to poke around Google Books, the Internet Archive, and other scanned repositories. But since I'm creating print-resolution works, I need to work from actual paper sources . . . so once the research has pointed me to a particular title or volume of a title, then I look on eBay! You can get great stuff if you're not too picky about condition (which I'm not). Weird stuff pops up in used bookstores too, but that's strictly luck if it does. Allow for serendipity, but it's good to put in the work as well. Also, important note: 1922 is the latest publication year where you can be absolutely certain the material is in the public domain.

Okay, thirty-second elevator speech: why should people read Wondermark?

If you think that life is fundamentally ridiculous, and you like staring through slightly warped windows to watch the wobbly world beyond, you might like *Wondermark*. I didn't mean for that to come out quite so alliterative, but I think it can only help my case so I'm sticking with it. *Wondermark* is by turns silly, sarcastic, incisive, and good-natured—just like YOU.

Any last words?

That prompt sounds very ominous! What do you know that I don't?

THE UNICORN QUEEN SPEAKS

BY SAMANTHA HIGHFILL

A self-identified unicorn queen, Doe Deere is famous in the fairy tale world. She's the creator of the highly successful Lime Crime Makeup and she keeps her fans up to date with her very own blogazine. A model and entrepreneur, Doe Deere works hard to "spread glee" to those around her. Here are some of the questions Quail Bell could not resist asking her:

What is it about the fairy tale world that fascinates you the most? Why?

My interest in fairy tales began early on—most kids grew out of it, but I never did. The world of fairy tales is the world where anything is possible, and that's how I want my world to be! I love fairy tales of all kinds—ancient and new, silly and deep—as long as there is magic of some sort, I'm in!

There is a quote on your site that reads, "Doe Deere Blogazine is like the fairy tale book of the blogosphere." When you read that, what is it saying to you? What does being a "fairy tale book" entail?

I thought it was very accurate that someone described my blog as that. As a child, I used to pretend to have magical abilities—to fly and make things happen on purpose. Most people leave such fantasies behind once they hit the age of twelve, but I continued on thinking I could (albeit in a different sense). I believe in the power of imagination and will and making things happen for yourself even though they might seem impossible at first.

My blog is part style, part makeup, and part inspiration for young women to keep dreaming and keep chasing their dreams.

You're also a fairy tale rock musician. Can you describe what that genre is for our readers? What was it about that music that pulled you in?

I used to play in a band called Sky Salt (defunct as of 2006) and we described our music as "fairy tale rock." My voice is of the breathy, "ethereal" variety, and we incorporated sounds like that of a music box into our songs. You can check out our album, *I Believe In Fairy Tales*, on iTunes.

What was it about fairy tales that inspired you, among other things, to create Lime Crime Makeup? How did you get your start?

I carried on with the magical theme for Lime Crime because it's true to my own life. I didn't see a lot of quality bright colors; in fact, had trouble finding them. So I decided to magically create my own. I got my start by researching what makes eyeshadows more or less pigmented—turns out, it's the cheaper ingredients like talc and kaolin clay—and decided to try making eyeshadow without them. By excluding them completely, you get pure, saturated color that goes on true to what you see in the box.

Lime Crime was born in late 2008. We carry sixteen eyeshadows from blue-black (amazing for smoky eye!) to bright sunny yellow! Last fall we came out with a line of opaque lipsticks that give you true, undiluted color—we even have a bright blue called "No She Didn't!"

Can you tell our readers a little bit about Lime Crime Makeup?

Its mission is to encourage women of all ages and walks of life to experiment with makeup. Lime Crime is a revolution in color—we're here to break down the norms of what's accepted as 'beautiful' and 'normal.' I believe that color is a natural anti-depressant and that people who incorporate it into their daily lives live happier, longer lives. It is also a fantastic way to express your colorful personality!

Makeup has been taking itself too seriously for way too long. We want women to have fun with it again without sacrificing the quality—inside that purple packaging adorned with a sparkling unicorn is top-notch product of professional quality (in fact, Emmy-nominated makeup artists use it and so do celebs like Katy Perry, M.I.A., and Cat Deeley).

What advice would you give others who are trying to get into the fairy tale world and be successful?

Believe in yourself and enjoy what you do! If you can see it (in your head), you can do it!

Do you have a favorite fairy tale? Why is it your favorite?

I have several, but my current favorite is *Harry Potter*. It's a story of a tortured boy with an unhappy past who follows his heart and overcomes it in the end. The classic tale of good and evil with a wizard twist. These books have changed my life.

What do you think needs to be done in order for the fairy tale world to continue to expand and touch lives?

More people with a vision and the drive to carry it out. There is a quote by Karl Lagerfeld: "Sometimes it's easy to have ideas, but somebody has to find a way to do it. Often those responsible for finding a way don't have the idea." We need more people with a pro-active approach to their dreams, who believe that IMPOSSIBLE reads "I'M POSSIBLE."

If you had one message to send to our readers, what would it be?

Keep following your dreams, and don't let anyone stop you! There will be people and obstacles that will try to slow you down or discourage you entirely, but don't listen to them. You have the right idea of what your life should be.

THE END

Dear Josephine Stone,

When you died on October 28, 2011, at the tender age of twenty-three, we lost a talented writer, enthusiastic managing editor, and dear friend. A shining star fell from the sky over Richmond, Virginia, that night. Then Destiny pinned it back to the velvet curtains, and Oderus Urungus's voice boomed, "You better give Josie everything she ever wanted." And since we knew you always wanted a book, we gave you one. Actually, we gave you two—*The Nest: An Anthology of The Real* and *Airborne: An Anthology of The Unreal*.

We dedicate both anthologies to you, wishing that they do justice to your creative gifts, aspirations, and memory. For your sake, we hope that death is better than life, but, as Tristan told Isolde, love is more than both. We love you, Josie.

Feathery hugs,

The Quail Bell Crew

ABOUT THE EDITORS

Julie DiNisio is a 2013 graduate of Virginia Commonwealth University. While still a student at VCU, Julie served as an assistant editor at *Quail Bell Magazine*. Now she is a Teach for America fellow in Memphis, Tennessee.

Christine Stoddard is a 2012 graduate of Virginia Commonwealth University. She founded *Quail Bell Magazine* in 2010. Now she runs Quail Bell Press & Productions, LLC, and writes full-time. Christine lives in Richmond, Virginia, with her sister.

www.ingramcontent.com/pod-product-compliance
Lightning Source LLC
Chambersburg PA
CBHW051307250626
47155CB00009B/3467